THE

EMOTELLIGENT

LEADER

Succeed Where Others Failed

Become the leader everyone loves and
wants to follow

KINGSLEY GRANT

ISBN
ISBN-13: 978-0-9884142-4-2

DEDICATION

This book is dedicated to leaders who want to succeed where others failed and want to be the leader everyone loves and WANT to follow.

CONTENTS

AUTHOR'S NOTE

I'm Kingsley Grant.

I'm a part of a group of LEADERS you've probably never heard of until you picked up this book. We believe that we've discovered the right mixture of ingredients that lead to increased productivity, team cohesiveness, and team satisfaction. These are the ingredients that leaders who failed wish they had.

The volumes and volumes of leadership books on the market make it very difficult for you to decide which ones will offer the most practical suggestions needed to become a better leader.

Research by the respected Center for Creative Leadership (CCL) in the U.S. found that the three main reasons for leadership failure are difficulty in handling change, inability to work well in a team, and poor interpersonal relations.

We believe we've found the antidote.

As you turn the pages, you will discover the 7 Essential Ingredients to becoming the leader everyone loves and wants to follow. Your confidence will soar like never before.

We call ourselves Emotelligent Leaders and we're inviting you to become one, too.

As the author of this book, I've discovered that the label of "High-Performing Leader" is one that is replicable. It's not just for a select few who boast about their IQ, but it's for everyone who desires to be a better leader.

I've been on both sides of the fence and have learned from the best and worst leaders.

Many of these leaders have had leadership training and may have had coaching as well, yet seemed to lack that one thing that would make them an exceptional leader.

The one thing I believe they lacked was their ability to work well with the people they were leading.

It's one thing to be given the title of leader, but it's quite another to earn the title of leader. A leader who fits the latter has embraced the spirit of "Emotelligence."

Emotelligence is the art of succeeding where others failed. It is sometimes referred to as "Hybrid Leadership" because it combines the skills of emotional intelligence and leadership to create a framework that differentiates it from other leadership concepts.

This is what you'll be exposed to within the pages of this book

CHAPTER 1

PERSPECTIVE MATTERS

A Camping Trip!

Sherlock Holmes and Dr. Watson went on a camping trip. After a good meal and a bottle of wine they lay down in their tent for the night and went to sleep.

Some hours later, Holmes awoke and nudged his faithful friend awake. "Watson, look up at the sky and tell me what you see."

Watson replied, "I see millions and millions of stars."

"What does that tell you?" Holmes questioned.

Watson pondered for a minute.

"Astronomically, it tells me that there are millions of galaxies and potentially billions of planets.

Astrologically, I observe Saturn is in Leo.

Horologically, I deduce that the time is approximately a quarter past three.

Theologically, I can see that God is all powerful and that we are small and insignificant.

Meteorologically, I suspect that we will have a beautiful day tomorrow.

What does it tell you?"

Holmes was silent a moment, then spoke.

"Watson, you fool. Someone has stolen our tent."

Author unknown

Emotelligence: the art of succeeding where others failed, will give you the right perspective on leadership. you will see what other leaders don't see, hear what other leaders don't hear, feel what other leaders don't feel, and know what other leaders wish they had known

CHAPTER 2

INFLUENTIAL LEADERS DIFFERENT OUTCOMES

Why is it that some leaders are able to easily get people to love and follow them while others have such a hard time doing so?

Is it charisma?

Is it their accent?

Is it their physique?

Is it their eloquence?

Is it financial?

Is it their possessions?

It could be any one of them or a combination that results in leaders being able to influence people to love and follow them.

As we look across history, we see many leaders who possessed one or more qualities found in the short list above and were able to move people to do things others were unable to do.

One of the persons that comes to mind is Martin Luther King, Jr. (MLK) His name comes to my mind right away as I'm working on this book because it so happens that I'm tapping away on my keyboard on the weekend of his birthday.

I do not have to restate, what so many have already done through their writings and other forms, the impact this one man had on a generation. Even after his death, his legacy still lives on. This is one sign of an impactful and influential leader.

MLK was able to marshal hundreds of thousands of people to conduct marches, sit-ins, peaceful demonstrations and the like, simply by the eloquence of his messages, charisma, and his willingness to do what he was asking those who followed him to do. He "rolled" up his sleeves and did it too, even to the point of being arrested numerous times.

There are many more like MLK who led people to do things that were constructive, productive, and empowering.

There are other leaders who had similar attributes and were able to amass a large following of people but led them to outcomes that were quite opposite.

The person that comes to my mind is Jim Jones who led over 900 people to their death in 1978. Some died by suicide, others by other murderous and violent means.

Why would people follow this man the way they did even to the point of dying for and with him? I know at the point where this murderous plot was underway, many of them had no choice. They were too far gone and it was almost impossible to turn back.

But what was it about Jim Jones that allowed him to sway the masses the way he did?

Like Martin Luther King, Jr, he had what it took.

He had the charisma, eloquence, and the message that resonated with his followers. He too was an influencer.

You might be thinking that a person who does not have "what it takes" is simply out of luck. They will not be able to become a leader everyone loves and wants to follow.

Here is where the surprise lies. A person who desires to become a better leader, makes changes, and learns new skills can become a leader everyone loves and wants to follow.

This is where this new paradigm of Emotelligence: The Art of Succeeding Where Others Failed comes into play.

The word Emotelligence might not be one with which you are familiar. As a matter of fact, you are not the only one. However, by the end of this book, you will be very familiar with the word.

As you might be able to tell by sounding out and looking at the word, you'll notice that it is made up of two words. The words are Emotion and Intelligence.

This process is called portmanteau, which is the joining of two words together that have their own sound and meaning. I learned this while doing research for this book.

Some examples are: smog (smoke + fog); brunch (breakfast + lunch), sitcom (situation + comedy), and infomercial (information + commercial).

Emotelligence is pronounced: EE-MOH-TE-LI-GENCE. It's the art of succeeding where others failed.

This paradigm is what makes it possible for someone who desires to become a better leader to make the necessary changes and learn the required skills to become the leader everyone loves and wants to follow.

You might be thinking this sounds so simple that it simply can't be true. You are operating by the maxim that says: "If it sounds too good to be true, it probably is."

Well, this is not the case here.

This is a tried and proven method. It has been tested with one-on-one coaching and live leadership training, which I have conducted. It's the Emotelligent Leadership training and coaching.

As you work your way through this book and things become a bit clearer to you, you'll agree with me that it is not as difficult as one would imagine.

Before you jump in, can I impress upon you the importance of having an open mind? It is impossible to learn something new if your mind is not willing to at least consider what it is you are open to learning.

Some people will embark upon reading this book to see what they can find to 1) confirm what they already know and to 2) overlook a new thought or concept that doesn't fit into their "box."

Don't be one of those people.

Be like the person who listens to a song and allows the song to soothe their soul without trying to take it apart key by key.

This doesn't mean you have to agree with everything that is written here. I don't expect you to. As a matter of fact, you should be challenged by some things you read. You will be provoked.

When you come upon sections that don't immediately resonate with you because it may be a new concept, remember that is what learning anything new is all about.

To normalize some of what you will probably experience from reading this book, let me share, in a succinct way, the path of learning something new.

There are four stages to learning something new that I'd like for you to glance over prior to embarking upon your book voyage. Here they are:

Stage 1: Unconscious Incompetence

Here, the learner isn't aware that a skill or knowledge gap exists. It's the "you don't know what you don't know until you know what you didn't know" realization.

Stage 2. Conscious Incompetence

Here, the learner is aware of a skill or knowledge gap and understands the importance of acquiring the new skill. It's in this stage that learning can begin. It's the "you now know what you didn't know."

Stage 3. Conscious Competence

Here, the learner knows how to use the skill or perform the task, but doing so requires practice, conscious thought and hard work. It's the "becoming better at what you didn't know but now know."

Stage 4. Unconscious Competence

In unconscious competence, the individual has enough experience with the skill that he or she can perform it so easily that they do it unconsciously. It's the "I now know and practice what I didn't know without any hesitation. It's like second-nature to me now."

If all of the "I now knows" are confusing to you, take heart, you won't be confused at the end of this book. You will be an Emotelligent Leader - the one everyone loves and wants to follow.

The key to this paradigm working is your willingness to do something about what you read. Don't simply be a hearer but be a doer of what you are reading.

This book is broken up into basically two segments.

The first is to introduce emotional intelligence to you in the context of leadership. It will not be like other books you may have read on the subject. Some of the other books give you a treatise on the subject. I don't intend to rehash what you already know.

The second segment will focus on outlining the framework on which Emotelligence is built. This could also be seen as the pillars of Emotelligence.

The framework is made up of seven attributes. They are Stewardship, Relationship, Partnership, Mentorship, Craftsmanship, Salesmanship, and Directorship. As you may notice they all end with the word "ship."

I sometimes refer to this framework as "The 7 Ships of Leadership," which was initially going to be the title of this book.

Each of these seven attributes will be peppered with emotional intelligence lingo.

I'll be citing and including the works of some of the leading experts on the topic of emotional intelligence, two of which are best-selling authors Daniel Goleman and Travis Bradberry.

My hope is that when you finish reading this book, you will label yourself an Emotelligent Leader. You will wear this "label" proudly as you make your "pledge."

You will be given the opportunity to make a commitment to a "code of honor" alongside other Emotelligent Leaders.

This will be an oath to the movement of raising up leaders everybody loves and wants to follow.

Capture your takeaway from this section below, and then read on.

TAKEAWAYS

Influential Leaders, Different Outcomes:

_____

_____

_____

_____

_____

CHAPTER 3

BETTER DECISIONS BETTER OUTCOMES

Does the name Captain Chesley Sullenberger aka Captain Sully, sound familiar to you?

What about US Airways 1549 that safely "landed" on the Hudson River in 2009 where the lives of 155 people were miraculously spared?

Would you agree that both Captain Sully and his co-pilot Captain Jeff Skiles, who were put in charge of this aircraft or any aircraft for that matter, earned the right because of their intellectual ability and skills?

What we can agree on is that both pilots have an average or above average IQ to have earned their pilot's license. They were both qualified but they did not have similar experience.

Captain Sully is a veteran pilot of over 40 years and nearly 20,000 flying hours, and co-pilot Jeff Skiles - even though a veteran pilot himself with 30 years of experience as a U.S. Airways pilot - had only recently completed his training on the Airbus A320.

Both pilots were very involved in bringing the airbus to a safe "landing" on the Hudson.

What does this have to do with becoming an Emotelligent Leader?

Everything.

What it took to land that plane is more than what it took to fly the plane. We could say it took a high IQ to fly the plane but high EQ (Emotional quotient) to land the plane.

There are a number of pilots who found themselves in situations where their aircraft was hampered by mechanical or electrical problems who were unable to do what these pilots did.

If you were to place these pilots into a category, would high performer be one of those categories?

This would be a no-brainer.

I've yet to have someone say otherwise during one of my presentations on The Emotelligent Leader. When I ask this question, there is a unanimous agreement by those in attendance.

TalentSmart, a research company, surveyed over a million people and tested their emotional intelligence alongside 33 other important workplace skills. What the agency found was that emotional intelligence is the strongest predictor of high performance, explaining a full 58 percent of success in all types of jobs.

What they also found from this survey is that 90 percent of top performers and achievers scored very high on the emotional intelligence surveys.

Emotional intelligence (EI) is a term that is used interchangeably with emotional quotient (EQ). Whenever you see these abbreviations, they are basically referencing emotional intelligence.

What is emotional intelligence and why does it matter?

Emotional intelligence is the ability to make healthy choices based on accurately identifying, understanding, and managing your own feelings and those of others.

This is one of many definitions of EI. You will come across another definition in later chapters.

You will find that most of the definitions used have the common thread of EI woven through them.

Imagine with me for a moment what it must have been like for Captain Sully as he took charge of the aircraft and guided it to a safe landing on the Hudson River.

Can you picture the intensity on his face? Can you see him doing all he could to hold his emotions in check to give himself the best chance of pulling off a miraculous landing?

According to an article I read that narrated the flight details of US Airways 1549, Captain Sully was in EI mode when he landed the plane. He did everything he could do to manage his emotions and the emotions of others, including that of his co-pilot Captain Skiles.

Twelve minutes into the flight, the aircraft's engines came to an abrupt stall, after encountering a flock of Canadian geese, making their southbound flight.

It was miraculous that the engines didn't disintegrate.

Captain Skiles tried to restart the engines. After his attempt failed, Captain Sully took charge of the flight and immediately communicated with the New York Traffic Control Center that they were turning around to make an emergency landing at the very airport from which they had taken off.

The plane began to lose altitude quickly.

With no thrust and a lower altitude, he decided that a turn to glide the plane back to LaGuardia, which is all the plane was now capable of doing, was not even a viable option.

Captain Sully had to make very quick decisions. He had no room for a do-over.

He had to maintain his composure knowing full well the implications. All it took was for him to lose his focus and logical reasoning and the situation would become fatal.

In a high-stress moment like this, the average person would be freaking out. I think I would be that person. What about you?

It is highly probably, normal even, in a situation like this, to be overtaken by your emotional brain. We call this an emotional hijack.

An emotional hijack is when information entering your brain, through what you saw or heard, triggers a fight, flight, or freeze emotional response. The emotional brain, also known as the amygdala, interprets the information as a threat to you and goes into protection mode.

This response short circuits the attempt for rational or logical thinking about what new information may mean.

Captain Sully had to reign in any attempts for an emotional hijack. He could not afford for his emotional brain to take charge of this situation, as life-threatening as it may have been. This was evident by what he did next.

He quickly considered his options and, having done so, communicated this message to the air traffic controller: "I am not sure if we can make any runway. What's over to our right? Anything in New Jersey? Maybe Teterboro?"

Teterboro Airport is a general aviation relief airport in New Jersey.

He was cleared to land there.

Within a few seconds of being cleared and having processed his options, he realized that the plane would not be able to make it there either. In his mind, this was no longer a viable option.

He radioed this message to the air traffic controller whose name was Patrick Harten: "We can't do it."

Patrick Harten thought that he meant he could not land on the cleared runway and replied: "Which runway would you like at Teterboro?"

The response from Captain Sully came as a surprise to him. What he heard next was not what he had expected. The reply was, "We're gonna be in the Hudson."

Captain Sully had made a decision.

Emotelligent Leaders who find themselves in a "do or die" situation make decisions that reflect conscious and careful thought for the safety of those whom they lead. In this case, the passengers and flight crew. He was responsible for them.

The passengers and the crew knew that something was wrong when the plane began making a rapid descent amidst the deafening silence of the engines.

However, during all this time, the captain said nothing to them. He was managing his emotions and thought this was the best way to manage theirs at the same time.

Sometimes we say more by saying less or nothing at all. This is one of the traits of the Emotelligent Leader, which you will learn more about as we unpack the seven attributes of leadership in later chapters.

Can you imagine the emotional state of air traffic controller Patrick Harten when he heard those words from the captain?

He had to ask the pilot to repeat what he thought he heard to make sure he was hearing correctly.

One of the thoughts that would have gone through my mind was a decision of a person who knew they were going to crash-land and possibly die, but would rather choose the river to do it in.

Captain Sully chose to use his mental energy to focus on seeing if he could miraculously land the plane on the river, rather than continue in conversation with air traffic controller Patrick Harten.

With his sights on the Hudson River and having no engine to help him along, he settled in for the landing. He had no idea what the outcome would be, but he was determined to give it his best shot.

He knew he had to clear the George Washington Bridge, which stood as one of his major hurdles. He had to cross this bridge first, no pun intended.

Leaders who are managing their emotions well understand this principle: do the first next thing.

It's a waste of time to use energy on matters you have no control over or on what comes next, before taking care of what is right before you and then moving on to the next thing.

Clearing the bridge was of utmost importance. What would it matter about the water if the plane didn't clear the bridge?

This does not mean you totally detach yourself from what is to come next. No! You are "eating the elephant one bite at a time."

In the entrepreneurial world, we call this reverse engineering.

It is working back from a desired goal to see the steps needed to get there. It is breaking down that goal into mini-goals and then tackling one mini-goal at a time.

The big goal here was to land the plane on the river. The mini-goals were made up of:

1. Making a decision to land

2. Setting the plane in the direction of the target

3. Gliding as long as possible to clear the bridge

4. Messaging crew to prepare the passengers for a crash-landing

5. Setting the nose toward the water

6. Slowing down as much as possible

7. Pulling up just in time to glide on the water.

I don't know if these were what Captain Sully had in mind, but I knew he was taking it one step at a time.

With about 900 feet to spare, Captain Sully cleared the George Washington Bridge and radioed the crew to prepare the passengers for a crash landing.

The crew shouted this command, "Brace! Brace! Heads down! Stay down!"

The delay in communicating with the passengers until the last moment was genius on his part.

Can you imagine what might have happened if he had alerted them any earlier than at this point?

Who knows!

Captain Sully knew his responsibility as an emotionally intelligent leader and as a high performer was to manage the situation as calmly as he could.

He succeeded.

He landed the plane safely on the river.

All 155 passengers, including the crew, were safely evacuated.

As a leader who cares about those entrusted to his care, Captain Sully was the last to leave the plane, making sure everyone got out first.

There are three major takeaways that emerge from this story as it pertains to being an Emotelligent Leader. You will see traces of this throughout the book. Here they are.

Emotelligent Leaders are better at:

1. Decision making

2. Managing Relationships

3. Higher Performance

We saw all these three traits at work in the actions of Captain Chelsey "Sully" Sullenberger.

These are traits that you too can possess. The good news of emotional intelligence is that it's a learnable skill.

Unlike IQ, which is very much set from early childhood throughout adulthood, EQ is not. It is a learnable skill.

Captain Sully isn't the only one who demonstrated his ability to manage his emotions and the emotions of those around him. I'm sure you could think of a number of people who you could point to as being an emotionally intelligent leader.

Like Captain Sully, I too made a split decision a few years ago, that might have saved my life as well as that of my wife and my son.

All three of us had gone to look at a car that was for sale that my son had seen in an advertisement.

The area in which the owner lived was not the best area in town. It was an area that I wouldn't want to live in, especially with young children.

Having looked at the car, I asked the owner if we could take it for a test drive.

He readily said yes.

As we drove down a side road, I saw a car quickly make its way out of a side street just ahead of us. It didn't come to a full halt at the stop sign. The driver of the car seemed like he was in a rush, so he cut out before me. This caused me to press harder on the brakes than I would have normally.

Not only did the driver "cut me off" but he immediately slowed down. This is one of my pet peeves in driving. If you are going to merge into the flow of traffic ahead of me, do one of two things: keep with the flow of traffic or go a little faster. But never, never, never, slow down.

What has kept me sane, especially driving in the city where I currently reside, is the fact that I pride myself on being an Emotelligent driver. You will get a chance to use this label toward the end of the book after making your pledge.

Before I had a chance to say a few choice words under my breath or out loud—good ones, of course—I saw some blue and red lights flashing behind me.

Immediately my thought was, "Yes, go after him. I'm glad you saw what he did."

With lights flashing behind me, I slowed down expecting the police car to whiz by me and pursue that reckless driver ahead.

To my surprise, the car before me had turned on its flashing lights. I now realize it was an undercover police car and I was the intended target.

I'm wondering, "What did I do?" I wasn't speeding. I hadn't gone through a stop signal or sign. So, what could it be?

Before my mind could even settle on any one of the possible reasons, I saw two officers pointing guns at us and barking orders: "Put your hands where we can see them!"

Quickly, we complied.

The officers, still having the guns pointing inside the car, bent down and looked in.

Then, based upon whatever criteria was used, they put their guns away and apologized for what we just went through.

One of the officers proceeded to tell us that the car we were driving fit the description of one that was used in a crime recently and, they thought for sure, this was the car.

We explained how we came to be in the car and were taking it for a test drive. They believed us and told us we could go.

We thanked them and, after having exhaled and breathed a prayer of thanksgiving, we drove off.

What if I had not managed my emotions and the emotions of my family and the police officers, I probably would not be here today. Imagine, you would never even be reading these words or know anything about me. This last sentence was placed there to lighten the moment. So, smile.

How was this story similar to that of Captain Sully?

The same three Emotelligent attributes were displayed.

1. I made a good decision in following instructionsp wouldn't you say?
2. I managed the relationships around me – my family and the officers
3. I performed my "job" at the highest level.

As you can see, EQ is essential for our daily functioning, even at times, in potential life and death situations. The good news is that Emotional Intelligence is a learnable skill. You will see how this plays out even more in the following chapters.

In the meantime, here are some of the summarized benefits of EI especially as it pertains to a workplace or in a team setting.:

- It helps leaders motivate and inspire good work by understanding others' motivations.

- It empowers leaders to recognize and act on opportunities others may be unaware of.

- It assists in the recognition and resolution of conflicts in a fair and even-handed way.

- It produces higher morale and assists others in tapping their professional potential.

TAKEAWAYS

Better Decisions, Better Outcomes: _____

_____

_____

_____

_____

_____

CHAPTER 4

POSITION OR PERMISSION LEADERSHIP

Is it possible to become the leader everyone loves and wants to follow? Do you know anyone who is like that? Is there a leader in your life currently or in the past whom you've loved or admired and followed?

What were the qualities that this person had that attracted you to seeing them the way you did and made you want to follow them?

The leader that I've loved and want so much to follow is Jesus Christ. You may not be a believer in him or a follower of his, but if you are an honest person, which I believe you are, you cannot deny the fact that he was a one-of-a-kind leader.

Millions of people have agreed with this assessment of him and have raised their hands to follow him.

There are other leaders who come to mind and everyone has their favorite.

Some would argue for Mohammed, Gandhi, Mother Teresa, Margaret "Iron Lady" Thatcher, Martin Luther King, Nelson Mandela, just to name a few. This list could be an exhaustive one if this book was about listing the names of great leaders, but it's not. I'm sure someone somewhere has attempted to do that and, if they have, may have left off the names of those important to others.

Again, we all have our preferences.

The one thing that can be said is that these leaders were leaders of influence. They influenced and continue to influence the masses.

Leadership guru John Maxwell is known for repeatedly making this statement -- "leadership is Influence."

His stance is that all leaders are influencers. We either influence people in a positive way or a negative way.

I have seen both the positive and the negative influence of leaders. Haven't you?

You and I know of people who have led multitudes or are leading multitudes in the wrong direction such as the Jim Jones type we discussed earlier. I'm sure there are some who alleged that we are doing something similar.

We have seen or experienced this across various platforms: spiritual, political, cultural, just to name a few.

So many people are following leaders who don't even know where they are going. It's the blind leading the blind.

Do you know of anyone like that?

Another teaching of John Maxwell that I like is the "5 levels of leadership." The two that I like most are the first two levels.

THE EMOTELLIGENT LEADER | 33

- Level 1: Position

- Level 2. Permission

In the first one, he talks about the fact that people follow the positional leader because they have no choice.

They do it because they are told to do so. It is the way to receive some sort of compensation.

In the business world, you could think of that as a paycheck. You follow the positional leader because you want to get paid.

You do whatever you are told to do because your leader says so.

As you may realize or have experienced, this kind of leadership doesn't get much mileage. It will get an element of cooperation from those who are being led, but only an element — not the full cooperation that they're hoping for.

They do so with their less-than self. They leave their best selves outside the door.

According to Gallop, 87 percent of people are either actively disengaged or simply disengaged from their work.

This means that they are only doing the bare minimum.

Even though the organization is doing well, imagine what could happen if these followers were fully engaged?

Another frightening statistic shows that people join organizations because they like the organization. There is something about the organization that attracts them and they feel like they should be a part of it.

However, these same individuals leave those organizations - not because they fell out of love for the organization — but because of a leader.

What some leaders tend to do when this happens is to blame the people who are leaving. They'll make statements like these: They were not committed. They aren't loyal. If they were committed and loyal, they wouldn't leave. They are an unhappy bunch of (expletives).

Many of these leaders haven't taken the time to look in the mirror. Maybe, just maybe, the reason they left is because of their leadership or lack thereof.

This is why leaders need to become more emotionally intelligent.

Not only will this help them in their own leadership skills, but it will also help create an environment where people are more inclined to stay and bring their best selves to the workplace or wherever they're asked to show up.

How would you like to lead a group of people who give their best in service and become your biggest fan, translating that fanship into organizational loyalty?

If you don't want this, you should not be leading. Why else would you accept the position of leadership?

The second level of leadership, according to John Maxwell, is Permission Leadership.

This level has to do with relationships.

He makes the point that the better you are in relationship-building with those you lead, building it into the culture and environment, the better it will be for everyone. It is the most important factor for increased productivity and retention.

People follow you because they feel like you have earned permission to lead them. This level of leadership sets the stage for successful and effective leadership.

It is the level where you have been granted permission to lead. The question is, "How do you get this permission?"

Most of the "how" is covered in the chapters on "Leadership is Stewardship" and "Leadership is Relationship."

However, suffice it to say, you as a leader must not take it for granted that your position entitles you to lead.

Many leaders who have held the title of "leader" failed in leading because they had, what I call, an Entitlement Mindset.

They simply assume that people fall in line because of their position.

Many of them have had a rude awakening to the fact that leadership, especially in the 21st century, doesn't work that way.

Being intentional to build good working relationships with your team is where it all starts. I say a lot more about this in the "Leadership is Relationship" chapter.

The takeaway that I want you to have from this section is that you must abandon the mindset of entitlement. This is where it all begins — with you.

TAKEAWAYS

Lead from Position or with Permission: _____

_____

_____

_____

_____

_____

CHAPTER 5

EMOTIONS MATTER

One of the first reactions that I've had from some people when discussing this topic is — "Is this just about feelings?"

Somehow this seems to be an issue, especially for some men. It's as if having an emotion or showing your feelings is something that's bad.

I do understand it, primarily because I was one who grew up in a culture that didn't highlight emotions in a positive manner — especially as a male.

I grew up in the "boys don't cry" generation. In essence, it wasn't O.K. to show your emotions. Keep it to yourself, they said. To display emotion as a boy, you were told to stop being a girl. Confusing, right?

You were also told that to show your emotions is to show weakness. So, it was quite common to associate showing your emotions as weakness.

So, I understand when I get the reaction from some who question the idea of leadership and emotions. It's as if the twain should never meet.

Maybe you had that thought initially.

I hope as you work through these pages, beginning with this one, you'll have a different perspective at the end.

Having said that, it is important to understand that emotions are important for effective leadership. It's impossible to be a leader that everyone loves and wants to follow if you are not in touch with your emotions and the emotions of the people you are leading.

How often have you heard of leaders who are "out of touch" with their people? When you hear that, what does "out of touch" mean to you?

Yes, it can mean that they don't seem to understand what their people are going through within the workplace.

It can also mean that some leaders have forgotten what it meant to be led by someone else.

But I believe the most important message is that some leaders are not sensitive to the emotions of the people they are leading.

To be in touch emotionally means that you will be able to empathize with what is going on in someone else's life, namely your team members or staff. From this point on, I'll use the term team members to refer to people you are leading regardless of where they fit within your leadership role.

Not many leaders are emotional intelligent enough to know how to lead, guided by their emotions.

Many are able to do so with their intellect, which is why they obtained a leadership role in the first place.

What some studies have shown is that the higher up you move on the leadership ladder, the more you'll need to be emotionally intelligent.

Why?

You will be depending on people more to get the work done. Your people skill is paramount for your success at this level. Hence the need to become an Emotelligent Leader.

But before I share with you the process, let me continue with why this process is not about being emotional.

As I mentioned earlier, some leaders have a hard time putting the words emotional and leadership in the same sentence. To do so conjures up weakness, which is one trait they want to stay as far away from as possible.

Why?

It's the word emotional. Who wants to show their emotions as a leader?

It's interesting that this word when used in a leadership context takes the position of weakness. It is seen through a negative lens and it's almost always associated with shedding tears or simply tearing up.

Is that what comes to your mind? You're not one of those, are you? I really don't think you are and that's why you are reading this book.

Let's be clear, we all have emotions. We express emotions daily. As a matter of fact, I've heard some people say there are upwards of hundreds of emotions that we experience daily, while others say thousands.

I'm not sure if we can pin down a number. But, suffice it to say, there are a lot.

However, these "lots of emotions" are derivatives of a few basic emotions. What we experience stems from them. The prevailing thought is that there are six basic emotions: anger, disgust, fear, happiness, sadness, and surprise.

I would even narrow those six down to four: Sad, Mad, Glad, and Scared. I wish there was a word that I could insert instead of scared to keep the flow going. If you can think of one, make sure you leave that as a feedback when you offer your review about the book, which I'm hoping you would. Even if it is a suggestion, I may include it in an updated release and give you credit for it, if you'd like.

If you were to recall the three basic colors: Red, Yellow, and Blue, every other shade of colors stem from these three basic colors. Some estimates state that there are over 10 million shades of colors. Imagine that. All of those colors come from three basic colors.

That's what I'd like you to think of when we use the word emotions. Whatever number of different emotions there are, they all stem from these four or six basic emotions.

Why did I take time to mention the colors?

It's to give you a reference point when we discuss emotions. It's important for you to know that emotions come in all sizes, shapes, and sounds. How one person expresses their emotions may not be the way another person expresses theirs.

You don't want to paintbrush everyone and see them through any one lens.

We all have what's known as unconscious bias, which simply means we behave in certain situations based upon our predisposition in judgement.

For instance, if we use the baseline of expression of tears to conclude that someone is sad or grieving, our unconscious bias will create for us a lens that looks for tearful expressions, when we think of sadness and grief.

But I would bet that you know people who grieve and show sadness without the shedding of tears. These people tend to be looked upon suspiciously because they are not grieving "properly."

I have been guilty of that at times prior to me becoming more emotionally intelligent.

As you can see, being emotionally intelligent will require you to go the extra mile. Yes, on top of what you have to do, this cannot be neglected or be less of a priority.

Your sensitivity to your team members' emotions will be key to your success. You will be loved by all when they see you taking time out to be empathetic to their situation and making the effort to do something about it.

This does not mean that you are using emotional display to curry favor. We are not naive to think that everyone is being genuine when they are emoting. Unfortunately, some will use their emotions for manipulative reasons. But you want to err on the side of grace.

The question arises, how do you manage your emotions during these times as well as the emotions of your team?

This is where emotional intelligence enters the scene.

You might be asking, the question at this point that many others have asked, which is: what is emotional intelligence?

I will give you two different definitions and will tell you the one that I like best.

The first one states that emotional intelligence (EI) refers to a person's abilities to perceive, identify, understand and successfully manage emotions in self and others.

The second one, which is the one I use most often - especially when I'm conducting The Emotelligent Leadership Training - states that EI is your ability to recognize and understand emotions, and your skill using this awareness to manage yourself and your relationship with others.

One of the reasons why I like the second one and use it more is the emphasis on the word "skill." This word suggests that you can develop the ability to become more emotionally intelligent, because like any other skill, it can be learned.

One of the recommendations that I will make here is that if you want to figure out where you are on the emotionally intelligent scale, you might want to take one of the many emotional intelligence assessments that are available to you.

The one I took was from Talent Smart, a company that administers tests and resources on EI.

Founder of Talent Smart Travis Bradberry wrote a book as a follow up to Daniel Goleman's book on EI and he entitled it Emotional Intelligence 2.0. When you purchase a new copy of his book, there is a sealed envelope in the back with a code that you can use to go online and take the EI test.

It is not the most comprehensive EI test, but it meets the requirements for having a base-line from which to work when it comes to your EI development.

What I like about the book is that it gives you practical ideas, based on your results, as to what you can do to improve in the areas where you need development.

There are four domains of emotional intelligence. They are more often referred to as the "4-Quadrant Model," made popular by Dr. Daniel Goleman. He is accredited with taking EI to the marketplace through his best-selling book of the same name.

The four domains are Self-Awareness, Self-Management, Social Awareness and Relationship Management.

Self-Awareness has to do with the understanding of your own feelings, what causes them, and how they impact your thoughts and actions. This is foundational to all the others.

Self-Management has to do with the ability to control impulses and to manage your internal resources such as adaptability, flexibility, self-control, and accountability. These resources are helpful in your ability to manage your emotions.

Social Awareness is having an awareness of the feelings of others and considering those feelings in your response both in words and actions. It's mostly about empathy.

Relationship Management is the ability to use awareness of your emotions and the others' emotions to manage interactions successfully. It is the culmination of the first three.

You might be wondering what this has to do with you becoming the leader everybody loves and wants to follow ... everything.

Let's break it down by starting with Self-Awareness.

TAKEAWAYS

Emotions Matter :_____

_____

_____

_____

_____

_____

CHAPTER 6

SELF-AWARENESS AND LEADERSHIP

A re you aware of your feelings, what causes them, and how they impact your thoughts and actions?

Here's the thing, if you are like me, our feelings happen so fast that we tend to react before we have time to think in a rational manner. Am I right?

Have you ever behaved in a way that after having had time to reflect on it, you wished you had reacted differently? Have you ever had to agree with someone who pointed out a negative behavior in you and suggested that you could have behaved better?

I have.

What happened?

There is a term again —emotional hijacking.

When we are triggered by something that happens to us, our emotional brain hijacks our ability to think rationally. That part of our brain is for our protection. It is where we receive the message to flee, fight, or freeze.

Think of a time when your spouse, staff or someone said something to you that immediately sent you into a defensive mode. Do you have that scenario in your mind?

Now, do you recall what you were thinking?

I would imagine one of your thoughts had to do with protecting yourself - your reputation, your position or your manhood. You felt threatened.

It's your emotional brain that sensed the threat and sent the signal to react in a "fight" mode to protect you from "harm."

Your awareness of this pattern allows you to be in a better position to guard against behaving in a manner that negatively impacts those around you.

It's important to know that your mood sets the tone for the overall organization. Your team and others close to you will do their best to avoid you when you are in this "mood." They tiptoe around you. They avoid having conversations that could directly affect the bottom-line of the company.

Imagine, someone having a critical piece of information that could make the difference between having a positive outcome versus a negative one but, because of your mood, they kept it to themselves.

Why?

The fear of what you might say or do. To them, you are unpredictable. This is where it's not about having emotions because of what someone said or did, but how do you manage them? This is the self-management piece.

Remember what we said self-management was? It was your ability to practice self-control by becoming more adaptable, flexible, and accountable. But you cannot manage what you aren't aware of and to take it a bit further, being willing to acknowledge.

Here's the thing: emotions, you will have. They are inescapable. We all have them. We are emotional creatures. No one is exempt from them. But are you aware of them and know where they're coming from — their source? The source makes a difference.

How so?

If I were "offended" by someone who I don't give a rat's tail about, then I could easily chalk that up to a moronic behavior on their part and move on. They are a "nobody" to me.

Before you think I'm calling people names and looking down on them, I'm not. It's just a harsh way of framing it to move past it quickly and more easily.

On the other hand, if it is someone who is more meaningful to me, then I will need to approach it more tactfully.

One way to do that is to look past the singular "offense" to be able to give this person the benefit of the doubt. Maybe it was your interpretation of what was said or done, which as a psychotherapist, I can tell you is more often the case.

We assign meanings to our experiences as we see fit. We also add labels, which makes things bigger than they actually are. It is to these that we react and not so much what actually happened.

Our reactions to these incidents can have a chilling effect on those around us. We will deflect our anger at the people who had nothing to do with it in the first place.

It's the old familiar story of the boss who yells at his wife. She gets home and yells at her husband. Husband, in turn, yell at his daughter, who yells at her brother who ends up kicking the dog.

The dog gets the worst of it and the sad part of the scenario is that he had nothing to do with it. It's called deflection.

That's what tends to happen when you are not able to be self-aware and practice self-management.

TAKEAWAYS

Self-Awareness & Leadership:_____

_____

_____

_____

_____

_____

_____

CHAPTER 7

SOCIAL AWARENESS AND LEADERSHIP

Social Awareness is having an awareness of the feelings of others and considering those feelings in your response both in words and actions. It is built on the emotion of empathy.

As stated earlier, it is very difficult to tune in to the feelings of others and be considerate of them, if you are emotionally ignorant.

Your people are dealing with issues that they take with them to work. It could be issues relating to their marriage, children, health, finances, grief, and so on, but you'd never know as you ought to, if you are out of touch emotionally.

There is a quote that has been attributed to a number of people. I'll assign it here to anonymous. It says, "Be kind, for everyone you meet is fighting a battle you know nothing about."

How true this is. I can guarantee if you were to take a poll of your team members and ask how many of them are experiencing a challenge of some kind in their lives, you'll find that more than half of them would raise their hands.

It's amazing how some of these members show up each day with a heavy heart. Maybe some of them are feeling lonely even though they are among people. Maybe they're anxious, scared, fearful, or a host of other emotions.

They do it because they have to work and some of them do it just to keep themselves busy. They do a great job of covering it up until something happens and they become a mess — unable to function.

But because you have developed your self-awareness and are able to identify your triggers, you are more inclined to feel for others. You know what it's like to be in "pain" and go through the gamut of emotions. You've been there and felt that, so you are able to feel for others when they are in their pain.

Have you ever watched a sporting event on television and looked at the face of a disappointed athlete who may have been the favorite to win their event but was beaten by someone else?

Do you recall how you felt looking on the emotions being exchanged and managed?

In 2018, I watched Naomi Osaka defeat the "Goliath" of women's tennis - Serena Williams - at the US Open finals. Many people were rooting for Serena to win because she was making her way back from being a new mom. She was on a mission.

Most people expected her to win even though she was out of the tennis circuit for quite a while.

Even though an unfortunate turn of events involving a shouting match between Serena and the referee overshadowed the achievement of this 21-year-old phenom, when the trophies were being presented, Serena graciously accepted her second place trophy and, like a champion should, congratulated her rival who had beaten her.

You could see Serena doing everything to manage her emotions. The tears flowed while she spoke mixed in with a smile. It was hard to watch.

Having played soccer and experienced a major loss at a national championship game, I know how it feels to lose.

Even though these were two different events, one - a team sport - and the other - an individual - the pain of loss is similar.

I empathize with Serena. I felt her pain even though I didn't care who won. I'm not a huge tennis fan. I was drawn into it at the last minute as I channel-surfed the cable stations.

Even if she had not said anything, I was able to identify with her. Pain recognizes pain.

As a leader, you too will be able to pick up on the emotions of your team members, the more self-aware you become.

When you do, you'll be much better prepared to manage the relationships with your people. They'll take notice and sing your praises even though that wasn't your motivation.

TAKE-AWAYS

Social Awareness and Leadership :_____

_____

_____

_____

_____

_____

.

CHAPTER 8

LEADERSHIP HAS A PRICE

G etting a title and a position of leadership is easy.

Many people today who are called leaders have no business being in that position. They don't know how to lead and can become a liability to an organization.

Starbucks experienced this reality in 2018.

STARBUCKS: A 16 MILLION-DOLLAR LEADERSHIP BLUNDER

One of Starbucks' leaders, who held the title of a manager, made a decision that cost the company about $16 million. Imagine, sixteen million dollars for a poor decision. But, not only that, it was a decision that jeopardized the overall company brand.

It happened when a video went viral after two black men, who were inside the cafe waiting on someone, were arrested. Millions of people saw the video and heard about what happened.

According to the news account, the men were waiting there to meet with another person to discuss business matters, as is customary at Starbucks stores.

They were denied use of the bathroom because they were not patrons of the store and were then asked to leave.

When they refused to leave, the manager called the cops who came, arrested them, and led them out of the store in handcuffs. The men peacefully cooperated and were escorted out.

The video brought national attention to the racial component that was raised. Starbucks realized they had to do something quickly.

The unnamed manager/leader was removed from her position at the store. CEO Kevin Johnson made a statement on behalf of the company along with offering an apology to the two men.

He said the manager acted in a "reprehensible way." He went on to apologize for what happened on ABC news as well as outlining what Starbucks will do to try and remedy the situation.

He said, "clearly, there's an opportunity for us to provide clarity and in addition to that I'd say there's training, more training that we're going to do with our store managers, not only around the guidelines but training around unconscious bias."

The question is, did Starbucks promote this person to a leadership position without proper training or vetting?

What did they miss?

Could this have been avoided?

I'm not sure of Starbucks' process for promoting someone to a leadership position, but it's obvious that they missed something here.

But I don't want to focus on the Starbucks policy and what they did or didn't do right. This book is about the leader and, in this case, the manager — what she did or didn't do right.

It's obvious that she didn't handle this situation correctly. While there are definitely some racial issues at play, I will focus on a simpler issue to diagnose — a lack of emotional intelligence.

One thing I would say, and that is, she would not meet the criteria of being an Emotelligent Leader who everyone loves and wants to follow.

Whatever she felt about the men and them not purchasing a menu item from the store, she failed at the crucial point of managing her emotions correctly.

I'm sure they were not the first nor will they be the last to sit inside a Starbucks store without purchasing an item. While I've almost always made it a point to purchase at least a coffee, I too have sat in on rare occasions when I was merely meeting someone there.

If you recall, the working definition that we are using throughout this book on emotional intelligence is that of understanding your own emotions, managing them and managing the emotions of others.

This leader failed because she may have felt:

- disrespected
- threatened
- dishonored

Who knows!

But whatever her feelings, they needed to have been managed more appropriately. As someone rightly said, it is not so much what happens to us, it is how we respond to what happens.

She was emotionally hijacked. Her emotional brain took over.

She used her position to leverage against these men. It became a power struggle and she was determined not to "lose" this one.

Have you ever experienced this tension?

I have and, may I confess that, I have failed miserably at times.

One of the reasons I believe I'm very qualified to write this book is not so much because of my professional expertise, even though that is a plus, but also from what I've learned from my failures as a leader in my home and at the workplace.

I have leveraged my title and position to get "my way" and it did work temporarily, but I can assure you that some of the times I was building walls and didn't even realize it until it was too late.

When you have to resort to leveraging your title or position to get things done, it could be an indication that you don't have the right kind of relationship with the people you are serving.

I remember hearing a statement by Josh McDowell many years ago that said, "Rules without relationship lead to rebellion." I have never forgotten that.

When people feel like you are pushing the authority card, they push back, at times directly, and at other times, indirectly.

They will not give you their best selves and this is something you cannot control.

Yes, you can threaten and use other tactics, but you won't get their best selves.

I remember hearing a story about a little boy whose dad became frustrated with him because he wasn't listening. His dad barked out, "Sit down!"

The little boy slowly sat down staring his dad down but said nothing.

When the little boy was asked what was going through his mind when his dad shouted at him, his answer was, "I'm sitting down on the outside but I'm standing up on the inside."

That is what you'll get from those you are leading who feel like you don't have permission to tell them what to do.

"Permission," you say. "Who needs permission? I am their leader. They do what I tell them."

This may have been your thought when you heard the word permission being mentioned.

It's important to realize you are trying to lead people and not machines or robots.

There is an old English Proverb that I grew up hearing that is very fitting here. It says, "You can catch more flies with honey than with vinegar."

When you take the time to build a relationship with your people, you are engaged in honey manufacturing. You are telegraphing to them that they matter and that you care.

These are the small deposits you are making in the bank of the relationship that entitles you to withdrawals when the time comes.

Many leaders are trying to make withdrawals from their people without making any deposits.

Here's something else to consider: leveraging title and position, keeps you at arms-length from your team. Who wants to be around someone where the perception is that they don't care about their people? I sure wouldn't. Would you?

I'm going to share something with you that you may not ascribe to, which is quite okay. Even if you don't, make sure you don't overlook the principle.

SERVANT LEADERSHIP

The greatest leader of all times, in my opinion, is Jesus Christ. One of the many leadership lessons I've learned from him is the way he led without using his title and position to get him ahead. He could have easily leveraged his title as Son of God and position of Second Person in the Trinity, but he didn't.

According to the sacred texts, he didn't allow his title or position to get in the way of him building relationship with his followers. As a matter of fact, he did things that were revolutionary.

- He washed their feet as a servant.

- He cooked and served them breakfast as a host.

- He shared sleeping space with them, as one of them.

- He sat on the ground with them as one who wasn't above them.

These are just a few of the many things he did as a leader, which marveled his followers. This was such a shift from what they had seen from many of the leaders of the day that it captured their attention.

His leadership style resonated. His followers had no doubt that he cared for them and wanted the best for them. They knew it. They felt it. Is it any wonder they gave him their best and admired him so greatly?

Let me hasten to say that not all thought well of his style of leadership. Of course, there were haters along the way. I'm not naive to think that everyone will see this kind of leadership style as admirable.

When you decide to become an Emotelligent Leader, you too will have haters because you are going to be doing things differently from many of your peers. Doing this will "show them up."

When I have shared this idea, I've had some pushback from people who think that this kind of leadership that I'm suggesting is too much work. Some will say that they don't have the patience for it.

Here's one of my response to that: "What are your alternatives?"

Yes, you can continue leading as you do and get the results Gallup shared in a poll on workers and job performance. What this poll showed is that 64 percent of people are disengaged in their work. Twenty-three percent are highly disengaged in their work. This tallies to 87 percent of people who are showing up to work simply because they have no other choice right now... a paycheck.

Imagine that.

So, the alternative to being an Emotelligent Leader because of the work involved, which really isn't much as you will see through this book, or the time it takes, is having a group of people who are leaving their best selves outside the door.

What then is the solution?

I'll be talking more about this and giving more practical examples of what this would look like, under the chapter on "Leadership is Relationship."

In the meantime, focus on being a honey manufacturer and dispenser.

TAKEAWAYS
Leadership has a Price: _____

_____

_____

_____

_____

$$\boxed{\text{CHAPTER 9}}$$

LEADERSHIP IS STEWARDSHIP

S tewardship?

"Never heard of it," you say.

If that is your immediate reaction to the word stewardship, you're not the only one. I find a similar reaction from a number of leaders at my Emotelligent Leadership Training when asked if they've ever heard of the word stewardship within the context of leadership. Not many raise their hands. Some even stated they've never heard of it.

We're going to change all that.

Stewardship in leadership is one of the most important and foundational traits of successful leaders. The word stewardship according to Merriam-Webster first appeared in English during the Middle Ages.

It functioned as a job description, denoting the office of a steward, or manager of a large household.

In recent years, the long-established "management" sense of stewardship has evolved to a more positive meaning, "careful and responsible management."

The latter definition is commonly found in contexts such as "stewardship of the environment, family business, etc." (Merriam-Webster online dictionary)

Stewardship, according to Vocabulary.com, means the management or care of something, particularly the kind that works. If your company is making money, there's probably been careful stewardship — or, a lot of luck.

If I were to ask you to choose leadership words from these two definitions, I hope you would have chosen the following: management, manager, care and responsibility.

The sphere or responsibility of a leader/steward is often used to mean "the care, handling and management of ..." It's about "Taking care of those in your charge" rather than focusing on "being in charge." People want to know how much you care.

The question is, how much do you care and how do your people know that you care?

If they were to be surveyed, what would you hope their answers might be? I hope you are not one who has the "I don't care" attitude. That "I'm the boss" attitude. I hope that is not your attitude, which I don't think it is, merely from the standpoint that you are reading this book.

With that said, think of the answer you would like them to give, and begin to work back from that point. It's the late Stephen Covey who said in his classic book: The 7 Habits of Highly Effective People, "Start with the end in mind."

As you work backward, outline the steps it would take for you to get that kind of feedback and start implementing each step along the way.

The first time I came across the word steward was when I read it in the Bible. It was used by Jesus as he told the story of a business owner who gave his manager (steward) a task of taking care of the staff and workers until he returned.

When the boss - the owner - returned, he found out that the manager -the steward - had failed to carry out the tasks he was given.

He fired the steward/manager for failing to care for the staff and workers as expected of him.

This story is found in Luke chapter 12 toward the end of the chapter. You won't find the story written as I have just described, but you will find the principles outlined there.

Whatever you come up with, may I suggest that it should begin with the five domains of caring.

CALLED TO CARE

As a leader, you need to think of yourself as someone who has been entrusted with the care, responsibility, and the management of those you are leading and that one day, you're going to have to "give account" of how well you led them.

This "giving account" may not be that you get "fired" in the way the manager/leader did in the prior story. You might be the business owner/leader and don't have to fear that. However, don't get too comfortable with that thought, and here's why.

Those you led may have resulted in your firing as one by one they chose to leave your domain of leadership and take their skills and talents with them. In essence they've "fired" you.

If you are not the "owner" of the company, your boss may have no choice than to replace you because your leadership or lack thereof may have led to lower productivity or perhaps some of the best workers have left because of you.

When you adapt the role of a steward-leader, you are simply taking the position of leading with the people in mind. You are saying that you are going to be the leader who recognizes that you have been entrusted with caring, managing, and safeguarding what's in the best interest of those you are leading.

You may have heard this phrase before: People don't care how much you know; they want to know how much you care. Teddy Roosevelt is credited with that quote.

The late Maya Angelou once said, "I've learned that people will forget what you said, people will forget what you did, but people will never forget how you made them feel."

Showing people that you care about them as a person more than you care about what they do will get them to want to give you their best work. This doesn't mean that you don't evaluate their performance. They understand that you will have to do so at some point. But what they want to know is "do you care about them?"

It's always good to remind yourself that you are entrusted with this privilege of caring, managing, and safeguarding the welfare of people.

I remember, after having learned as a teen to drive on my own while living in Jamaica, my dad entrusted me with caring for, managing, and safeguarding his fairly new car as he handed me the keys to go and pick up my sisters from a nearby school.

The pick-up point was about a mile away from where we lived. This was the drop-off point for my sisters who were being transported from the all-girls school they attended. It was four miles away.

Normally, the custom was that they would walk home from the drop-off point. However, on this day, my dad sent me to pick them up because of the bad weather we were experiencing. It had pretty much rained all day.

To my dad, that car was like a brand-new Mercedes Benz. Imagine being given the keys to such a car.

The car was a 1972 Ford Cortina. It was a beauty at the time.

Being asked to do this "small" deed, made me feel very special.

As I left home, I began to think of how I could make sure "everyone" saw me driving. By everyone, I meant the girls in the community.

Living in a rural area like I did, it was very uncommon for a teenager to be driving a car. Only a few families owned a vehicle. We happened to be one of them.

One of the thoughts I had was to find a way to get the most exposure as I could out of this brief, unique, and one-of-a-kind opportunity.

What I decided on doing was to drive the four miles to the all-girls school where my sisters attended and make sure as many girls at the school saw me.

This was a risky move since my sisters could easily have been on the way to the drop-off point already or were already there waiting for a break from the rainfall.

I had to make up for time to pull this off.

I drove to the school and made sure I got out of the car and asked a few girls if they saw my sisters. I knew my sisters were not there but it gave me a chance to talk to a few girls and be seen driving a car. To them, it was my car and was not going to convince them otherwise.

Knowing that time was of the essence, I didn't linger too much longer. The point was made and I was now on my way back to the drop-off and pickup spot.

It wasn't five minutes after leaving the school that I lost control of the car, hit the embankment, and flipped the car on its side.

A combination of the wet road, my speeding to make up time and my inexperience were not a good combination, as I found out.

My heart seemed to stop as the realization of what just happened set in. I was in shock but not for long.

I climbed out of the passenger side window and jumped to the ground. I wanted the earth to open up and swallow me whole. I didn't want to process the thought of going home.

"What would I tell my dad?!"

"How could I make up a good enough story for him to believe my reason for driving four miles instead of one?"

These and more questions and worst-case-scenarios were rapidly flashing through my teenage mind. I ran for help as quickly as I could.

These were the days when cellphones were not even on the radar.

The first home I came to, I knocked on the door and, in rapid-fire speech tried to explain what happened, and at the same time ask for help.

With the help of the homeowners and others who had stopped by to see what happened, we were able to turn the vehicle over so that all four tires were on the road.

Thank God there were enough people there who were determined to help me. Some of them knew my dad. That was one of the good things and not-so-good things about living in a small, rural community ... everyone knew each other or so it seemed.

I eventually made it home. As I drove into the yard, I saw my dad sitting on the front porch waiting for me. My sisters had all made it home.

Slowly, I made my way out of the car and, even slower still, walked up to where he was. I felt like I was walking the plank to an execution of some sort.

My dad immediately noticed the car and wanted to know what happened.

I did my best to tell him my concocted story.

Whether he believed me or not, I never knew. All I knew is what followed—a beating and a lecture. I can't remember which one came first. I was in the twilight zone.

Other than the side mirror being broken and dents and scratches on the side of the car, it was drivable. My dad eventually repaired the car and it was a very long time before he trusted me with driving his vehicle again.

I failed to manage, care for and safeguard what I was entrusted with. I got "fired!"

For me to have done a better job of managing, caring for, and safeguarding what was entrusted to me - my dad's car - I would need to make it less about me and more about his trust. My self-centeredness got in the way.

Many leaders fail because of this very thing ... self-centeredness.

Self-centeredness and leadership are two concepts that are diametrically opposed to each other. It's impossible to achieve success where other people are involved when the attention is primarily placed on self.

In thinking about stewardship as the key leadership quality, I took the liberty of looking up a few traits found in my favorite resource—the Bible, to see some of the qualities that exceptional leaders need to possess.

Here are a few excerpts I found in the books of First Corinthians and Titus.

An exceptional leader who succeeds where others failed possess the following qualities. He or she must:

- Not be arrogant or quick-tempered
- Not be a drunkard or violent or greedy for gain
- Be a lover of good
- Be self-controlled
- Be upright
- Be disciplined
- Be found trustworthy

Imagine being a leader with these qualities or having a leader who possesses these qualities.

Who would not want to work for someone who isn't arrogant or quick-tempered but is self-controlled, disciplined and trustworthy? Sign me up.

Before we go any further, which of the qualities above would you say that the people you lead would use to describe you?

I would have eliminated myself from being seen as this kind of leader because of what I did with my dad's car. Not only was I not safeguarding, managing or caring for the car he entrusted to me, I disqualified myself as a trustworthy leader.

I was not leading my life marked by that trait. My dad would be the first to raise his hand in agreement to this confession.

How about you?

What would the people you are leading say about you? Which of those seven traits listed above would they put a checkmark against?

You might want to pick one or more and do some self-evaluation. Be honest with yourself or you may want to ask a member of your team for an honest feedback.

Even though I mishandled what was placed under my care, my dad's car was used to illustrate the point of stewardship. It is unable to adequately highlight the personal aspect of leadership as stewardship.

People need more personal attention. The complexity of leading people requires more. It's an ongoing learning process. It is a fluid relationship. You are interacting with living organisms whereas the relationship with caring for a car is a more static and one-directional interaction.

The good news is that the "five domains of caring" approach will give you a framework to create a better and deeper relationship with your people. This framework is called the PIERS Framework.

THE P.I.E.R.S APPROACH

In caring for your people, these are five areas that I believe you must address to succeed where others failed. To overlook any one of these is to not fully care for them.

The five areas are

1. **P** - Physical

2. **I** - Intellectual

3. **E** - Emotional

4. **R** - Relational and

5. **S** - Spiritual.

Don't freak out on the last one. I'll explain when we get to that particular one. No need to sign up for a class on spirituality unless you want to.

PHYSICAL CARE

How do you communicate to your team members that their overall physical health is important to you?

As you know, the health of your team is unequivocally one of the most important aspects of their performance, productivity, and consistency in showing to work.

A 2016 report by Safe Work Australia, a government agency that develops and evaluates workplace safety laws, found that employers who prioritize productivity over employee well-being lose on average $6 billion a year—about US$4.5 billion—due to higher levels of employee absences as well as lower levels of employee engagement and commitment.

According to the report, workers in less psychologically healthy environments took 43 percent more sick days per month and were significantly less productive when at work, equating to $1,887 per employee per year—which converts to about $1,400 in the United States—in cost to employers, she says. (American Psychological Association)

Imagine what it is costing your organization when one or more of your team members are not in good physical health.

So, the question was, "How do you communicate that physical health is something that you pay attention to?"

If you are a large company and can create a work-out room where team members are encouraged to take advantage of, that would be one way.

You could give incentives for working out and/or weight loss, encourage members to participate in a challenge of some sort, and even give exercise breaks.

Another way is to make sure that members take stretch breaks where they are not seated for more than 90-minutes at a time. This could be modified as it relates to the type of work being done.

However, you as the leader must set the example. You don't have to be in the greatest shape of your life but making your physical health a priority will give you the moral authority to speak to the issue of physical health.

There are other measures that could be taken. We cannot cover everything here but being health conscious will give you the creative ideas of how to make physical health a priority.

INTELLECTUAL CARE

Do you provide opportunities for your people to improve their skills and education? What about continual training? How are you challenging your people to make intellectual growth an important aspect of the culture you are trying to create?

The more your people pursue personal development, the better it will be for you.

One of the reasons for hesitancy in some leaders to do this is that they fear developing their people intellectually, only to have them leave their organization and take those developed skills somewhere else. Their hesitancy or fear is often a reflection of their insecurity.

The thought is, "What if I train them or get them the training and they show me up and possibly replace me?"

I like this quote attributed to Henry Ford: "The only thing worse than training your employees and having them leave is not training them and having them stay."

Another way of saying this is, train your people too well and they'll leave — but don't train them at all and, lucky you, they stay.

Think about that for a second.

Do you want to have people on your team who are untrained and unskilled to the level you wish they were, and you refuse to train or get them the training they need?

Do you see how your "insecurity" hurts you in the long run? Not to mention the stress that comes with that. By the way, I'm not suggesting that you are insecure. It's the other leaders who need to read this book, I'm referring to as insecure ... not you.

Take a look at the large multi-national beverage corporation PepsiCo. They introduced training and coaching of emotional intelligence among their employees and leaders. The result was a 10 percent increase in productivity and a whopping 87 percent decrease in turnover, saving them $4 million with an ROI of over 1000 percent. (Dr. David McClelland, Journal of Psychological Science, 2008).

Training your staff to become more emotionally healthy pays dividends in their lives and in the life of your company.

I like what Richard Branson, founder of Virgin Group, said about helping your people grow. He said, "train them well enough so they can leave. Treat them well enough so they don't want to." This is how visionaries and secure leaders think. This is how Emotelligent Leaders think.

This concept is not easy.

It can make some people really nervous, thinking you could lose some of your best players.

Newsflash: If you don't train them so they have something to challenge them, you'll eventually end up losing them. It won't be long before they move on to some other place where they can grow.

Some of the ways that you can help them develop intellectually is give them access to as many resources as possible. You could do in-house training by inviting someone like myself to do a half day or a full day training. But you could also have them attend growth-oriented workshops.

In fact, a study by McClelland in 1999 showed that after supervisors in a manufacturing plant received training in emotional competencies such as how to listen better, lost-time accidents decreased by 50 percent and grievances went down from 15 per year to three. The plant itself exceeded productivity goals by $250,000.

One of the many things I admired about one of my past bosses is that he would pay for his key leaders to attend a national conference that focused on leadership of some kind.

This would include travel expenses, hotel accommodations, food, and access to the event. Granted, it was a costly endeavor, but here is what happened. We -the leaders who went- bonded at these events. It was more than just getting away to learn even though that was the central focus. It was also important for building more intimate relationships with our team.

The message that was communicated to us all is that he cared that we grew in our leadership skills and team-building skills. Knowing this, led to most of us remaining with the organization for many years.

What also excited me was that there were partial reimbursements for continuing education expenses incurred on our own. I, for one, enrolled in classes at local colleges.

Knowing that there were partial reimbursements, this added to my longevity at the organization.

These are some ideas you could implement that reflects your commitment to the intellectual growth of your people.

EMOTIONAL CARE

I came across this quote that is attributed to Anonymous, whoever that is....just kidding.

The quote captured for me the starting point for us as leaders when it comes to caring for our members in an emotional way. The quote states: "If you are not aware of your own emotions, you won't be able to manage them because they will constantly take you by surprise."

If you recall, the core component or skill of emotional intelligence (EI) is self-awareness. Self-awareness is your ability to accurately perceive your emotions and stay aware of them as they happen. In other words, you must be able to read, understand, and regulate (manage) them.

This is where most leaders fail.

As we discussed earlier, for whatever reason, some leaders do not make the connection with leadership and emotions. Some simply don't want to because of the perceptions or stigma in their mind, on emotions in leadership. The two should not be mixed.

Leaders who think this way, will have a hard time motivating their team.

A survey by Cigna Health of more than 20,000 U.S. adults ages 18 years and older revealed some alarming findings.

- Nearly half of Americans report sometimes or always feeling alone (46 percent) or left out (47 percent).

- One in four Americans (27 percent) rarely or never feel as though there are people who really understand them.

- Two in five Americans sometimes or always feel that their relationships are not meaningful (43 percent) and that they are isolated from others (43 percent).

These are just a few of the findings, yet they make a good case for you to look out for them in people on your team.

Without being emotionally engaged, alert, and aware, you will miss a wonderful opportunity to be the "hero" to your team.

Being able to spot members of your team who are struggling emotionally will be a plus for you. It elevates you as one who cares for them as a person.

To be able to do this, it requires that you become more socially aware, which is one of the four skills of EI.

Social awareness is your ability to accurately pick up on emotions in other people and understand what is really going on. You need to be skilled at this.

Here are a few ways to increase your social awareness.

- Be in tune with people's body language. If need be, research the meaning of certain types of body language.

- Check in with what you observe by asking questions to confirm your suspicion.

- Listen for tone within a conversation that betrays the words being spoken.

- If and when you notice that a member of your team is struggling with emotional issues, and having confirmed such, encourage them to get professional help. Maybe you could offer to pay for one or two sessions to get them started.

- If their situation is not too serious, recommending resources such as books, audiotapes, videos, workshops, etc, would be a good start. It shows that you care.

- You could also invite a professional to do an in-house training on helping your people identify and manage their emotions.

So many people have such limited emotional vocabulary that they do not know how to articulate their feelings. Some have even stopped themselves from feeling. By raising the awareness and making space for members to learn and share their emotions, you will unwittingly be helping to create a more emotionally intelligent culture.

RELATIONAL CARE

Do you provide opportunities for people to build relationships within your group?

So many people are starving for relationship.

An article from the National Health Service website entitled, "Loneliness, increase risk of premature death" states that loneliness can be fatal, almost at the rate of obesity and smoking.

Imagine, some of those people are on your team.

These are the people who have given up hours of their day to help you and your organization become all that it can be. Some of these people joined your organization with the hopes of building relationship with like-minded people. For some, this might be the only time they have adult interaction or any interaction for that matter.

Relationships build a sense of belonging and self-worth. It allows us to engage, grow, and develop communication skills. It also allows us to learn, to share space with others and not be as self-absorbed as some leaders are.

There is a contagious effect from being around people who possess a strong mental wellbeing. This helps others who might not be as mentally strong to become healthier. It is an "iron sharpens iron" effect.

By providing opportunities for your team members to connect with other members, you are providing them an opportunity to be healthier. The healthier they are, the better they are able to perform their work. Productivity and morale increase as a result of a relationally-minded environment.

Obviously, it has to be closely monitored.

There are lots of ways to build stronger and closer relationships. Here are a few.

- Create moments for team members to work together on projects, eat meals together, play together, etc.

- As previously mentioned under physical care, having workouts or weight loss campaigns could also serve to build stronger relationships.

- Any team-building activity where members are encouraged to work together is a great way to do this.

Here's a word of caution: do not try to force team members to do anything they do not want to do. Some people, because of their personality type, may find this to be too much for them. Your job is to be the best salesperson on this concept. We will discuss how to be better at selling in the chapter entitled: Leadership is Salesmanship.

SPIRITUAL CARE

Caring for your people spiritually may not be something you would think of as a leadership responsibility. You may not even agree with this premise and so you may skip this section.

I would understand if you did.

But before you do, if that was your intention, remember what I said earlier: "Be open to learn new ideas and concepts." This doesn't mean you have to agree with everything you read or with any at all.

However, a leader who is going to succeed where others failed and be the leader everyone loves and wants to follow, will have to do things that are out of the norm. He or she cannot subscribe to the typical leadership models being presented by most authors who write or speak on the topic of leadership.

Is it any wonder many leaders who have read, listened to, been coached and consulted by leadership experts still end up failing at leadership? Could it be that most, if not all, say the "same thing?"

This is why, when I mention spiritual care, some leaders cringe, especially if they do not see themselves remotely caring about spiritual matters. If they don't see it as important for them, why should they see it as such for their team members?

Leaders who think this way miss the point of leadership.

What's the point?

It's not about you, the leader.

Remember, your focus is on the members of your team. They must know that you care about them in totality ... their overall well-being.

You might not see yourself as a spiritual person, but what if one or most of your team members see themselves that way? What do you do with that?

To ignore them in this area is to ignore them altogether.

I remember working at the United States Postal Service (USPS) many years ago.

As one of the newest employees, we were given shifts that the people with the most longevity didn't want. They had first choice and rightly so.

My supervisor would schedule me for Sunday mornings or for Saturday night shifts, which end at about 7:30 am on Sunday morning. This meant, I would be dog-tired when I got off work that morning.

I would try to explain and plead to not be scheduled for the late Saturday night shift or for Sunday mornings because attending church on Sunday was important to me.

He would indulge me this request most of the time but there were times he would not, especially around the Christmas holidays.

He was not empathetic to my spiritual needs. I would not go as far to say he didn't care. That would be a far stretch.

However, whenever he scheduled me on the late shift or on Sunday mornings, he would not get my best self at work those times.

I know this is not right, because as a Christian, I ought to do my work as unto the Lord. I failed at those times. Forgive me. Don't hold that against me.

My point is that he didn't see my spirituality as something of which he needed to be mindful.

I know it gets tricky when most of the members have a similar need. However, there are ways to still show that you as a leader care about your members overall well-being.

Chick-Fil-A is one of the most successful businesses operating in the United States. The founders made an early decision that no matter where their stores were located, they would not open on Sunday.

Many people in the quick-food restaurant world saw this as a crazy business decision. The numbers would say that Sunday is a day when most quick-food customers eat out and so, logically, Chick-Fil-A would miss out on this opportunity.

The founders would not be swayed and so they stuck with their idea.

Their philosophy was that whether or not their people were spiritually-minded or not, they wanted them to know that they cared about them in all areas, which included their spiritual life.

In fact, while Chick-Fil-A doesn't operate as many stores across the country as say some of the major fast food chains like McDonald's, they earn more per store than McDonald's, Starbucks and Subway combined. In fact, the average Chick-fil-A unit made around $4,090,900 in 2017. By contrast, the total sales for a McDonald's ($2,670,320 per unit), Starbucks ($945,270) and Subway ($416,860) is $4,032,450.

You don't have to be like Chick-Fil-A or agree with them on their policy of not opening on Sunday, but you cannot argue with their success.

There is one local Chick-Fil-A store at which I have lunch at least once a week, and I am constantly blown away by the service I receive.

Everyone that I encounter at that location seems to be happy about working there. They smile at you, treat you with respect, and are happy to serve you.

Sometimes I wonder how they are able to find these kinds of people who all seem to be shaped out of the same "nice" mold while you only need to venture across the street to a competing food joint and experience quite the opposite.

What's the difference?

Chick-Fil-A's culture.

And, Chick-Fil-A is not the only company that through connecting with their staff on a socio-spiritual element has seen sales growth.

Sanofi-Aventis, a pharmaceutical company, had a test group of 40 sales reps that received EI training. Those agents developed skills in social and emotional awareness and management by 18 percent, compared to the control group.

Additionally, the trained group of sales reps outsold the controlled group by an average of 12 percent or $55,200 each per month. Overall, this led to a $2.2 million per month sales increase with the trained group of 40 reps. The ROI was 600% or $6 for every dollar invested in training and coaching. (Cherniss, Emotional Intelligence in Organizations, 2003)

Becoming sensitive to your members' overall well-being which includes their spiritual life will be a game-changer to your leadership.

TAKEAWAYS

Leadership is Stewardship: _____

_____

_____

_____

_____

_____

CHAPTER 10

DESIGNING A SAFE CULTURE

Your overall goal as the leader is to establish a culture that reflects your overall objectives of team-mindedness ... unity and a safe environment.

Everyone should be aware and clear of what that means. To achieve this, you must be clear on what that looks like. You need to know it very well so you can communicate it very well.

This is where most leaders fail. They don't have a clear vision of how they want their team to "behave."

Does everyone in your team know of the culture you are creating? Do you know what culture you want?

Before we discuss 5 Ways to create an Emotelligent Culture where team members are more productive, satisfied, and engaged, there is one very central theme that must be established; people must feel safe.

This is the glue that holds everything together.

When people feel safe to freely express themselves, make mistakes, disagree with others, show their emotions, and do all this without retribution or judgment, they are more likely to give their best to their assigned duties.

Not many leaders make creating a safe zone for their people to be their authentic selves a priority. Is it any wonder that there are surprises when people have a chance to say how they truly feel or think?

Why?

They feel muzzled. They have learned it's best to say nothing or very little even though they could say a lot.

How do they learn this?

By watching how others who dared to be authentic are treated. They may have also experienced negative reprisals from attempting to speak their truth.

I once worked within an organization that provided us autonomy in how we worked. There were policies and procedures in place that provided a framework for us. And as long as we stayed within those guidelines, we were okay.

We had channels for which to communicate our grievances, suggestions, or anything that we thought was needed to make its way to upper management.

I recall on a couple of occasions that I chose to use the channels to share some suggestions I thought would make more sense for what we were doing … at least in my humble opinion.

This simple suggestion became an issue.

A meeting was called with me and a senior management representative to discuss what I had suggested. This was a surprise to me. I saw it as unnecessary and a waste of time. But I complied.

I left the meeting concluding that I would keep ideas to myself from that point on.

On another occasion, I shared my disappointment on how a fellow team member had managed or mismanaged, a client's situation.

This, again, did not go well.

It became a bigger issue than the last. Another meeting was called and, by the end of the meeting, I found myself defending myself against some false statements.

I remember taking some deep breaths, managing my self-talk to make sure they were positive, and said very little.

I left that meeting deciding that from this point on, I would show up, do what I have to do, smile at my team members, be cordial to them, but keep my feelings, suggestions and comments to myself.

Why?

The environment wasn't safe for me. I didn't know who to trust.

That is the way your team members will feel and behave when they do not feel safe to freely express themselves, make mistakes, disagree with others, show their emotions, and do all this without retribution or judgment.

So, having a safe environment is your number one priority. Once you've established that, you are now ready to add the other layers on top.

RECOGNITION

"People will work for a living, but they'll die for recognition"
~ Lee Olden.

Which of those among us would say they don't like to be recognized? We might all not like to be recognized the same way, but we do desire it. Even the most introverted person desires recognition.

According to Vocabulary.com, recognition is used "to describe when you remember that someone has done something special," and decide to recognize their efforts with an award or speech. This type of recognition is a form of acknowledgment, a way to say, "We approve" or "good work!"

Studies after studies have shown that people who feel better about themselves perform better than those who don't.

You can help people to feel better about themselves simply by recognizing the work they do. When you show your people that you see and appreciate the work they do, AND take the time to demonstrate how their performance is having a positive impact on the business and others, you've made them one happy person.

Not only will they feel happier, but they will treat those around them better because they are feeling happier. Happiness is contagious. Happy people make people happy.

An article in Fast Company cites a study by economists at the University of Warwick. The study showed that happiness among workers led to a 12 percent spike in productivity while unhappy workers proved 10 percent less productive. As the research team put it, "we find that human happiness has large and positive causal effects on productivity. Positive emotions appear to invigorate human beings."

I can attest to the link between productivity and recognition both as a leader and as an employee.

I remember working at a bank in South Florida where I made a suggestion that led to a more efficient and cost-saving way of doing a task within my department. It was so well received by management that they rewarded me with a $1,500 bonus.

Not only was the bonus a recognition of my effort, but it was announced in a public manner. My boss took the time at a meeting to make mention of it. I was applauded by my co-workers as well as management.

I don't know how I kept my head from exploding as the feelings of pride overwhelmed me. I graciously received the award. Everyone knew I was a happy camper. My smile almost split my face in half. IT FELT GOOD.

This happiness continued for the remainder of the day. I left work feeling happy and took that feeling home with me. Everyone who I interacted with knew that I was feeling something special ... happiness.

As a leader, one of the reasons that the majority of my volunteers and paid staff remained on my team for most of the years I served them was me taking the time to recognize their efforts. I did that through public and private recognition, respect for them, and tons of gratitude for their service.

It works.

The O.C. Tanner Institute, a research group, cited some very startling findings.

In one of their surveys, they asked employees (without prompting): "What is the most important thing your manager or company currently does (or could do) to cause you to produce great work?" Thirty-seven percent of the respondents gave this as their number-one answer: "Recognize me."

Imagine, it wasn't more money, promotions, or other perks like flexibility and more open space like some of the trendy and profitable companies are now doing. Some are thinking that productivity is the result of the latter.

This survey shattered those beliefs. As a matter of fact, the second highest response was, "Nothing, I'm self-motivated." And that was at 13 percent. Pay me more was at 7 percent.

The error that some leaders make is that they think they know what their people need or want. They just assume that if it worked for them as leaders, then it must also work for their team. This is so not true, especially in the 21st century workplace.

The survey went on to show that 78 percent of employees were more engaged in their work when they received strong recognition.

What are some ways you may recognize your team?

- A special framed certificate
- A VIP parking space for the month
- Spotlighting them in a company newsletter that goes out to employees
- Giving them shout-outs as often as possible

These are just some ideas. I'm sure you're able to find other ways that fit within your company's culture.

Creating a culture where recognition is given a high priority will be a game-changer.

SUPPORT

Sending and resending the message of the importance of each one supporting one is one of the most important messages you can send to your team members.

Crafting your message around what's in it for them is the way to help them to buy in. You'll read more about how to do this in the chapter on Leadership is Salesmanship.

One of the ways to do that is to help them see how a team's win is also an individual's win.

You may want to incorporate some team-building games to help them experience what it's like to do a task as a team. Choose a task where it cannot be done without the help of others.

There is a YouTube video that I've seen where some guys are given the task of scaling a fairly high wall. It is one that requires the help of others to scale. This was a timed competition.

What this team of guys did, once they were given the go signal, was to have two guys run to the wall and kneel down with their hands extended before them on the ground. Their backs would serve as a launching pad for the others.

The remaining guys sprinted toward where the first two guys were kneeling and, without breaking stride and in one sweeping motion, stepped on the backs of the kneelers then jumped up and grabbed the top of the wall.

Once they had a good grip, they pulled themselves over.

The last two did the same, and instead of hauling themselves over the wall, they left their legs dangling so that the kneelers could grab their legs and using their legs as a "rope" climbed up to the top and over the wall.

They all made it over within minutes. They had practiced for this, so they had it down to a science. That's team work. They all celebrated together.

This is what can happen when you give your team a chance to work together on a project. They will figure out how to "climb their wall" as they create a supportive culture.

APPRECIATION

Have you ever played the game where someone had to tell you three to five things they appreciate about you? If you haven't, you need to look up this game idea and have your team members do it.

This is a great way to build a culture of appreciation. You will literally see people transform before your eyes. It may lead to the shedding of tears during the sharing.

Here's how it works.

Get all or a group of your team members together and hand them three 3x5 index cards.

Randomly put them in pairs.

Instruct them to write three things about their teammate that they appreciate. Once they're finished, have them take turns reading what they wrote to the other person across from them.

You'll notice that many will struggle with this exercise.

Why?

It is easier to find negative things to say to or about others than it is to find and say something positive.

You could encourage them to find at least one statement of appreciation to share with one of their teammates over the next few days.

Here is the caveat: make sure you are doing the same thing yourself. It's important that you are not asking your team to do something you are not doing.

Find ways to communicate your appreciation for your team members. It could be something you say publicly, privately, in writing, through video, in audio, or any other form you are comfortable using.

But make sure you do it for all and not for your favorite persons. That would be a very serious mistake that could be disastrous.

RESPECT

This is another very important aspect of building a team-minded culture.

The late Jackie Robinson said these words and they still hold true today:

I'm not concerned with your liking or disliking me

All I ask is that you respect me as a human being.

Everyone wants to be treated with respect. As Jackie Robinson so aptly stated, to respect him is to treat him as a human being. A lack of respect is a devaluing of a person made in the image of God. And no one likes to be treated disrespectfully.

How do you create a culture of respect?

It starts with you as the leader.

Some leaders think that their team members should be respectful of them because they are the leader. In their mind, it's a given. It comes with the territory. They feel that no matter what, they should always be respected.

Granted, I do subscribe to the idea that the leadership positions should be respected. However, the person occupying that position may be one that isn't deserving of respect.

That leader might be disrespectful in the way they talk to and/or treat others. Maybe they are the condescending, racist, bigoted, sexist, all-around horrible type, which disqualifies them from being respected.

However, this cannot simply be because their haters say so. It has to be legitimate claims.

Most influential leaders have at one time or another been hated on simply because a group of people didn't like them because what they represented. Jesus Christ was hated by the religious sect of his day because he called them out on their hypocrisy. He was called names and treated with disrespect, simply because of who he was.

There are many others who experienced such treatment. My point is that you may experience this simply because someone doesn't like you. You cannot help this but it doesn't mean you should react in like manner. Successful leaders don't.

Speaking kindly to people, treating them fairly, praising in public and reprimanding in private, avoiding insults and sarcasm, are just some ways of modeling what it is you expect from your team members.

Being firm, vigilant, and intolerant of disrespecting behaviors is the way to create a respectful culture. But this starts with you.

GRATITUDE

If there was one thing that my parents would not tolerate, it would be ingratitude. We had to say thank you for everything we received. If we were having dinner together and one of the siblings asked for something to be handed to them, we had to say please and thank you. It didn't matter who handed it to us.

This was even more so if we received something from someone outside of the family. If my parents heard that we didn't say thank you, we would be in big trouble. If it were an item that we brought home, it would be taken away from us until we said thanks.

As a parent myself, I continued this practice with my children.

I recall on one occasion, one of my children received a Christmas gift. I asked a day or so later if they had made a thank you phone call. The child said no, so we took the gift away until they made that call. We were very rigid on this.

My parents wanted to create a culture of gratitude within our home and they were successful in doing so. My wife and I wanted to do the same and we were successful. At least I think so.

In both cases, the leaders in the home, my parents and my wife and I, had to model what we wanted. We led the way and, when we failed, we were called out, as well.

This ingrained behavior makes us very sensitive to ingratitude. When we are around others, we automatically expect them to say thank you when someone does something for them.

Because not everyone was brought up as we were, we are mindful of that and use that as our internal argument to empathize. However, we try our best to model gratitude when we can.

When I'm having a meal with friends at restaurants and the server brings us an item, I make sure I say thank you immediately, so that others will follow suit. It doesn't always work but I still do it.

I was at church one Sunday and the pastor had a cold. He was sniffling as he preached, and at one point, his cold was draining from his nostrils. He paused for a moment and asked his wife for a tissue. She was close enough to hand it to him.

However, before she was able to do so, someone else from the congregation beat her to it. He took it from them and continued to preach without saying thanks. That bothered me.

I turned to my wife who was next to me and said, "Did you see what just happened?"

"Yes," she said.

We both shook our heads and wondered who else noticed that and did they have a similar reaction to ours.

Imagine the ripple effect of that one action. It was amazing how I had to work hard to get my focus away from what just happened and back to his message.

This is what I believe happens within your workplace. Your team members are watching, especially those who are as sensitive to the gratitude issue as I am.

Imagine what would happen if you were to say thank you to your team members at every opportunity you got? What do you think would happen if, at team meetings, you took a few minutes to thank individuals and/or the whole team for something they did that made a difference?

Don't underestimate the power of your influence on your team members. What you say and do goes a long way.

Not only do you need to model gratitude to them, you also need to let them know that this is what you're expecting of them as they relate to their team members.

CONFLICT MANAGEMENT

Within any organization, one thing that you are sure to encounter is conflict. It is inevitable.

Some leaders see conflict as a bad thing and they try to do all they can to avoid it. This is more so if they have had very bad past experiences with conflict that didn't end well. So, this is understandable.

By reframing conflict as neither good or bad but simply as feedback, it gives you an opportunity to investigate the feedback and discover what is being said.

Have you ever noticed a caterpillar in "conflict?" It can look like a painful and exhausting process.

The conflict is called metamorphosis. It's where the caterpillar is going through the process of becoming a beautiful butterfly.

However, if you were to watch the process, there's very little beauty about it while it's going through this stage. I really don't even like to watch it. I am tempted to help the butterfly emerge from the cocoon that it is trying to break free from.

This conflict doesn't seem to be going well, but when managed carefully and without outside interference, the result is simply amazing.

Am I saying conflicts always end this way?

No.

Sometimes they are not managed well enough and the results can be disastrous as it would be if the caterpillar-to-butterfly conflict wasn't managed well.

Conflict can be a sign of growth.

When my children were maturing from teenagers to young adults, I realized that my parental approach had to be changed. I couldn't use the same parenting style that worked for them when they were younger.

The conflict came when we were negotiating curfew hours. Yes, they had curfew hours while they lived with us. That was our agreement.

However, the conflict was an indication that they were growing and needed to negotiate life more on their own without as much hands-on guidance from us as parents.

They were clear on our expectations but were free to negotiate within those guidelines however they chose. It was their life and they had to become more responsible for themselves.

Likewise, you as a leader, having set clear boundaries, as we'll discuss in the chapter on Leadership is Directorship, will see conflicts as a chance to provide and get feedback. It is a mutual process.

How do you show that you care when it comes to managing conflict within your department? Practice fairness, be self-controlled, and offer guidance through coaching.

Conflict should be seen as an opportunity to teach, train, and model, rather than something to dread or fear.

We won't know how much we've grown or are growing if we don't have a way to test what we've been learning through life experience or the training we have received ourselves. When we put our growth to the test, it can lead to conflict.

In every conflict, there are two or more people involved. When you hear the argument of one side, you are going to hear the victim's or the hero's rendition.

Be careful to not only listen to one side but to hear both sides. The ancient writings of King Solomon in Proverbs states: "The first to speak in court sounds right-until the cross-examination begins."

I love the words of James, the half-brother of Jesus: "Be swift to hear and slow to speak..."

The better you handle conflicts, the better able you will be to create a safe environment. Members will see the outcome and take note that they can be in conflict and not have disastrous endings.

MANAGING TENSION

Some leaders make the mistake of trying to solve tension. They feel anxious when tension exists. It eats away at them, especially if they are the type that wants to be in control.

Sometimes, I get like that. I don't like to feel tension around me. I want to fix it right away.

Have you ever walked into a room where you could just feel the tension present? I've heard it described as it being so thick, you could cut it with a knife.

How do you recognize it?

For the most part, it's by observing people's body language. The more self-aware you become in being able to read and respond to your emotions, you'll be better positioned to do the same when it comes to other people's emotions.

I like what pastor and author Andy Stanley said about tension. He said, "Tension is to be managed, not solved and you'll know it's tension when it's a recurring issue."

If you are able to acknowledge tension as something to be managed and not solved, it will allow you to step back from what you are feeling to take a more constructive approach.

What do I mean by that?

Take for example there is tension within your department at work, but you are not sure where it originated. You know it is present, not only because you are feeling it, but you are also seeing it by the expressions on your team members' faces.

Your knee-jerk reaction is to want to get to the bottom of it immediately. You don't like what you are feeling or seeing and maybe hearing.

If you were to step back and put your emotions on pause by taking a few deep breaths and centering yourself, you will be able to put yourself in a responsive mode rather than a reactive mode.

Your goal at this point is to make sure the tension is not affecting productivity or putting anyone in danger. Safety is paramount.

Once you've established that, you could calmly encourage parties to work toward a settlement where they own it.

Your goal is to manage it and let them "fix it."

MANAGING HURTS

One thing none of us can escape in life is being hurt. As long as we are interacting with people, we run the risk of being hurt. Sometimes this hurt is unintentional while at other times it is intentional or, at the very least, feels that way.

Have you ever been hurt by someone close to you? Someone that matters to you?

If you have, you know that type of hurt is the most painful hurt one can ever experience. When we can easily shake off the hurt done by someone who matters less to us, it is a whole lot harder to shake the hurt by someone close to us.

You are going to experience hurt from the people you lead at one point or another. It is only a matter of time.

This hurt could be in the form of unkind things being said about you, being let down by a trusted team member, being misunderstood, disrespect, or haters who deflect their pain on to you.

It's not that you are being hated that is really the issue, it's how you respond to the hurt that really matters.

This quote by Charles Swindoll is very fitting here. He states that "I am convinced that life is 10% what happens to me and 90% how I react to it." So true.

These hurt feelings are managed by your interpretation of what happened and the label you assigned.

Assigning the right label and placing a more helpful interpretation about what happens to you is not easy. It takes practice and a great deal of self-control. This is where having a high EQ comes in handy.

Not only will you be hurt by others, there is the chance that you will hurt others, as well.

You might hurt them in similar ways they hurt you.

They could feel let down by you, misunderstood, unfairly treated, ignored, dismissed, unheard, and more.

When I think about being hurt, I recall a quote by Mahatma Gandhi: *"Nobody can hurt me without my permission."*

To be honest, at first, I found it hard to know how to process this quote.

It sounds on the surface like I am responsible for my hurt. It is my fault to feel the pain the way I do.

However, taking the time to think it through, I can see what is being said. It goes along with what I stated about my interpretation or misinterpretation of the incident as well as the label I put on it.

By the way, a label is the word or phrase that I use to name the experience.

For example, I could say that the person who hurt me with their negative words is a bad person. Granted, they may be a "bad" person, but because I used that label, it is easier to find supporting evidence in my mind.

My mind will do a data scan to see what other information I have on that person to validate my conclusion.

Going back to the quote, I have to realize that I'm the one in control of what happens to me. I can choose to label the incident in a way that removes the personalization of it and see it as feedback that needs my attention.

The question is, how do we as leaders attend to the hurt we experience by a member of our team or when we hurt a member of our team? What should we do?

This is where self-management comes in handy.

We have to dig deep to respond and not react to what we are experiencing and to clothe ourselves with humility.

This is modeling time. The way we handle these moments is crucial to the creation of a safe environment for all.

Let me use a personal story to illustrate how we can approach these times of hurt.

Growing up in Jamaica with a dad who I cannot recall ever apologizing for things he may have said or did that brought hurt to us, robbed me of learning some very important interpersonal skills.

We/I had to learn how to feel hurt and navigate our/my way through it. This might have been a good thing to some degree in that we learned how to manage our feelings.

The question is, did we truly manage our feelings or did we learn how not to feel? The jury is still out on that.

Here's what I do know: I was unable to ask for what I wanted in relationships. I "sucked" it up, whatever "it" was at the time. I no longer had a voice or one strong enough to say yes or no.

Not only that, it was hard for me to take responsibility for hurting others. Even when I knew that my action caused hurt, I would try to justify or minimize my behavior. I became very prideful like my dad.

Until …

… Until the day came when I truly realized how much I had hurt my son. He was about 10 or 11 years of age at the time. Don't quote me on that. All I know was he was young — too young to have experienced how I reacted towards him.

As a parent, I didn't realize how much of how I was parented was playing out in my own parenting style.

Saying I was sorry to my children wasn't going to happen. Nope! No way Jose, whoever Jose is.

I'm the boss. I'm the leader. I'm the dad. Those I lead, namely my children, ought to understand that. I often leveraged my position of dad, boss, and leader to get the result I wanted.

But on this particular day, having shouted at my son who had behaved in a disrespectful way - at least in my opinion - to my wife, his mom, I wasn't going to have any of that, awoke me to this realization that I was behaving like my dad.

The consequence of my yelling didn't fit the crime of what he did. It was an overkill.

I did not immediately realize it. I was too heated.

However, after I calmed down and was no longer emotionally hijacked, it dawned on me how hurt my son was. I felt it.

I hurt him.

I had to decide what to do with what happened. Do I leave things as is and be like my dad, letting him "get over it" or was I going to step up and model effective leadership?

It took me a few hours to make the decision.

The decision I came to kind of surprised me because it was foreign to me at the time. I decided to apologize but not only apologize, but request forgiveness.

I revisited what happened and made sure my son understood what he did was wrong, which he did. I then made my move.

Up to that point, it was one of the most difficult things I was about to do. Remember, I didn't ever see my dad do it and, if other leaders in my life had done it, it's not the same as seeing your father do it.

What I knew were the words to use. They were "I was wrong, I'm sorry, please forgive me." Knowing them is one thing. Doing them is quite another.

Taking a few deep breaths, letting go of my pride by thinking more about my son, and centering myself, I tried to get those words past my lips.

For some reason, they felt stuck to the roof of my mouth. My tongue was in the way. Nothing was coming out. This seemed to have gone on for several minutes even though it may have just been seconds.

Eventually, I was able to get the first set of words out of my mouth.

I stuttered, "Son, I'm, I'm, I'm sorry for having uhm raised [swallowed], raised uhm, my voice at you the way I did." Yay, I got it out. I was making progress. After taking another breath, I stuttered, "I, I, I was wrong, would you please for, for, forgive me?"

Silence. Time came to a standstill. I waited for what I was hoping to hear from my very young son. It felt like an eternity.

The silence was broken by his voice. "I forgive you."

If it wasn't for the remaining residue of pride, I would have hugged him tightly, kissed his forehead, and bathed him with my tears. I was so choked up, I had to swallow a few times.

I thanked him and turned away. It was too much.

That was a moment I have never forgotten and it taught me how to truly apologize for hurting someone, especially those closest to us.

As leaders, we have these moments to model what it means to apologize, request forgiveness and take responsibility for our actions.

One of the questions I'm often asked is, "What if I didn't do it on purpose?"

My response is to use an analogy.

Imagine stepping on someone's toes even though you didn't mean to. It was an accident. You didn't even realize it until it was brought to your attention. What would you do then?

Would your first words be, "I didn't do it on purpose. It was an accident?" Or would it be, "I'm sorry, I didn't see your feet?"

I believe it would be the latter.

It doesn't matter that you didn't do it on purpose. What matters is that the other person brought it to your attention and you now have a decision to make.

When we are able to manage our emotions and the emotions of others, we position ourselves to be better leaders —leaders who succeed where others failed.

If we are on the receiving end of the hurt, we need to share with those who hurt us- stepped on our toes without knowing- what they did. They may not even have realized it.

Because you have modeled apology and given clear guidelines on what to do when one is hurt or have hurt another, you will have created a safer and healthier environment for your people to thrive.

The words of J.K. Rowling, "To hurt is as human as to breathe."

TAKEAWAYS

Designing A Safe Culture :_____

_____

_____

_____

_____

_____

CHAPTER 11

LEADERSHIP IS RELATIONSHIP

One of the most crucial aspects of leadership is the quality of the relationship they have with those they are leading.

There's a statement that I heard many years ago by author and speaker Josh McDowell that still resonates with me today. The statement is, "Rules without relationship leads to rebellion."

In a workplace setting, there are a number of rules - both spoken and unspoken - that workers are told to abide by. They are told what time to get to work, when to take lunch, and when to leave at the end of the day, plus a host of other "when to's."

To make sure they do, some companies have a punch card that workers are required to use to indicate the time they get to work, leave for lunch and leave for the day.

Other companies have some version of a card.

What they are saying is that they don't trust their employees to be honest with the time they say they've worked. I get it. Some workers are dishonest and have made it difficult for others who are not. It's the "good suffering for the bad" syndrome.

There are other rules that workers need to abide by. Some of which are unnecessary while others could be overbearing.

Some workers resent some of these rules, especially those that tend to question their integrity.

Leaders have to contend with this attitude which, in some cases, is no fault of their own. Many of them have nothing to do with the policies of the company. Yet they are being asked to enforce these rules.

This sets them up for a conflictual relationship with some of their team-members.

Leaders who are governed by emotional intelligence will make every effort to work within the parameters or boundaries they are given and find a way to build good relationships with their team-members.

They will do this in such a way that their team members no longer see the rules as an issue because, having a good relationship with their leader, makes the rules a secondary issue.

Even though the rules haven't changed, the relationship makes them less of an issue.

Another issue some leaders have to contend with is that of the prevailing thought of leadership.

Some team members simply do not trust leadership.

They are of the opinion that those in leadership do not have their backs and will throw them "under-the-bus" in a hurry.

Some of these beliefs are not unfounded. They are based on experiences either directly or indirectly.

As a leader, you have to contend with these issues that you may not have had anything to do with. They are inherited issues.

Building a bridge across these chasms can be quite challenging.

The good news is it is possible.

The question is how?

It begins with the "know, like, and trust" factor.

KNOW, LIKE AND TRUST

One of the most common phrases used in the context of business is this: "People do business with those they know, like and trust." I believe it is also true when it comes to leadership. Your people will do "business" with you when they get to know you, like you and trust you.

They are not just going to blindly walk in and give you credit on the knowing, liking and trusting scale. You must give them reasons to do so. You must earn it.

If I were to meet someone from your department and ask them what they know, like and trust about you, what would they say?

I know the knee-jerk reaction might be, "I can't help what people say about me!"

Reeeeally?

Okay, I will give you some grace to say you do have a point. People are going to make up their own version of who you are no matter how hard you try. But I do believe that is not the majority. Some will, but most won't.

Most will use the ingredients you give them to formulate a decision about you.

The question is, what ingredients are you giving them to formulate that decision?

Here's what I know: the more people know about you there's less room for misinterpretation. Your actions/behaviors will be better understood because of the context within which you're showing it.

One of my favorite quotes I've used in coaching or consulting is, "The more you know, the less you judge."

The more others understand you, the better your chance of them not misinterpreting or misunderstanding you.

For them to judge, misunderstand, or misinterpret us less, and to know, like and trust us more, there are a few things we can do to help them in that process.

Get to know them first.

What are you doing or what have you done to get to know your team members? How much time do you spend with them inside and outside your workspace?

I know of a new pastor who wanted to get to know the people whom he had been hired to lead. He was the "new kid" on the block. He was succeeding a long-term pastor-leader who had established a trusting and amicable relationship with those very people. They were loyal to him.

The new pastor understood he had a huge challenge before him but not an impossible one.

One of the things he did with some of the younger men was he joined them in playing basketball on an evening when they gathered to play a pick-up game.

He knew he was not in the best of shape and that he may not be able to keep up with the younger men, but that wasn't the goal. He wanted to be with them, play with them, and have fun with them and nothing more.

Yes, he had an underlying agenda, which was to shrink the gap between where he was and where they were... relationally. There is no better way to do that than through play. Yes, food is also another way, but playing is more effective because people tend to lower their guards during play.

This was a wise move on his part.

This was what I used in one of my leadership roles. I played with my team on numerous occasions as well as attended events and shared meals together.

When there is a large group of team members that you physically cannot get to be with all the time, seek out those you have identified as influencers, and build relationships with them. Let THEM get to know, like and trust you.

I found myself in a similar situation and I did the same thing. These influencers became my advocates and did most of the "work" for me.

Another way to do so is to assume the position of being a curious leader.

A curious leader is one who cultivates an inquisitive nature. It's not the kind of inquisitiveness that creates tension with others.

Instead, it's the type that makes others feel that you care about them as a person.

How is that done?

Make curiosity a necessary trait in your leadership repertoire.

BECOMING CURIOUS

Whenever I hear the word curious, my mind immediately goes to the phrase that I grew up hearing: "Curiosity killed the cat."

It was mainly used when you are trying to get more clarity or information by asking a question followed by another and, sometimes, another.

Most people who did not want you to know more than what they provided on the surface would use the "curiosity killed the cat" stop-card. This was their way of saying, "Don't ask any more questions."

I'm not sure if you grew up hearing this as well. I knew one thing: when I heard it, it stopped me in my tracks.

I knew immediately that I was not supposed to ask any more questions. Sometimes the tone used sounded like a threat. Having had at least one past experience where it was followed up by a physical blow to the body, it gave me reason to take heed.

What this did, at least for me, was stifle my learning at a deeper level.

It led me to assume a lot, make up my own story to things I could have simply found out by asking more questions.

As a leader, going "deeper" with your team by being curious is a necessity.

Doing so could be as simple as asking someone about their weekend to as elaborate as having someone complete a customized form with questions that are designed to give you insights into that person's life.

Imagine one of your team members coming in to see you first thing on Monday morning. They are following their normal Monday morning routine of getting information or directions from you.

Normally, you would treat the moment as a transaction where they ask you a question, you give them an answer or hand them something, and off they go. That's a transactional moment.

On this occasion, before you answer their question or hand them something, you decide to ask them about their weekend. And because you have been actively building a relationship with them, you ask them about their children and the party you knew they were attending, over the weekend.

What do you think would happen if you did that?

I'll tell you what would happen.

You would almost immediately feel a shift in the mood within the room. You would notice them relaxing their shoulders and softening their voice as they begin to tell you about their weekend.

The message you are sending by taking the time to do so is that they matter and you care about them in and outside of the workplace. You would have scaled up on that person's "know, like and trust" measuring instrument. Whether you know it or not, each team member has their own version of a measuring tool.

Being curious also requires that you master the art of asking open-ended questions.

Open-ended questions are questions that cannot be answered with a simple one-worded answer. If they are able to answer with a one-word response, it means you've asked a closed-ended question.

Here's an example.

If I asked, "Did you put the garbage outside this morning?" I'll more than likely get a one-word answer. It's either yes or no. That would be a closed-ended question.

However, if I asked, "What did you do about the garbage this morning?" I've now opened the question so that the response requires them to enter into a dialogue. This would be an open-ended question.

Curiosity is the key to deeper relationships. A deeper relationship is the key to becoming a more effective leader.

This is in no way suggesting that you cross the line in how you relate to your team members. Always maintain a professional decorum. Know your boundaries. Remember, you are still the leader who does not want to have your "hands tied" in making the tough decisions, which you'll have to make at some point.

In the chapter on Leadership is Directorship, you'll see why having boundaries in place and not blurring the line between leader and follower is so critical.

Because relationships are a two-way street, you want to have them be curious about you as well. You can invite them to do so by practicing self-disclosure.

SELF DISCLOSURE

This approach to build a "know, like and trust" relationship is not for the faint of heart.

It requires tact, humility, discretion, and appropriateness.

Self-disclosure, as the words imply, requires you to be vulnerable; you're going to disclose things about yourself others do not already know and, even if they knew, they're now going to hear it from you.

Not many people are comfortable with this method for building better relationships. You are going to disclose things about yourself that others could use against you if they so choose. This makes it risky.

However, I see this as one of those risks that is worth taking.

I love this quote by the Leo Buscaglia, the motivational speaker known as "Dr. Love" — "The person who risks nothing does nothing, has nothing, is nothing, and becomes nothing. He may avoid suffering and sorrow, but he simply cannot learn and feel and change and grow and love and live."

To get comfortable with disclosure, you might want to start with talking about areas of your life that make you feel just a little bit uncomfortable, enough that you won't "die" from.

You want to normalize talking about your vulnerabilities without feeling like you are going to die. You will become comfortable doing so over time.

The key is to do so only when it serves others and not you.

As a psychotherapist by training, when a client shares some heart-rending story with me and how difficult it is for them to get past it, I will sometimes share something of my life that lets them know that I'm not immune to pain and I have to work through issues, as well.

Many times, clients see therapists as people who have no problems. Why should they? They are the experts. They should know how to deal with life's pain and challenges.

That's how you are seen by some as a leader. You are the "expert" and have no problems in life. You are above their issues. You've got it all together. That is what some people think. Little would they know. Right?

Because they have this impression of you, when appropriate and in trying to make a point, share your vulnerabilities. This tends to level the playing field. They will feel you understand them and can relate to them.

Here are some areas that you can share about if you've had any experience: fear, loneliness, sadness, grief, apprehensions, doubts, etc. You can mention your experience with any of these as it benefits your people.

Here's a word of caution: Do not share simply to get their sympathy. This is counter-productive. Remember, it's not about you. It's about them.

BEING RELIABLE AND CONSISTENT

These two traits are very important in leadership. Your team members want to know that they can trust what you say and what you'll do. It makes them feel secure knowing that your yes means yes, and your no means no.

One of my favorite authors –James, the half-brother of Jesus - wrote these words over 2000 years ago: "A double-minded man is unstable in all his ways."

You don't want to be seen as double-minded. That's a sure-fire way of not becoming the leader everybody loves and wants to follow. Why should they follow you when they don't know if you are going to change the "rules" on them?

Here's what I know: How you do one thing, is generally how you do everything.

When you make promises, make sure you follow through on them. This helps to create a trusting and reliable relationship.

If you have to change your mind about something, make sure you take responsibility for why you have changed your mind.

There are indeed times when, due to no fault of yours, you will have to change your mind. This should be the exception and not the norm.

People understand that we are imperfect beings who will make mistakes. They will give you a pass on that.

However, when it becomes the norm, they'll conclude this is who you are and no longer expect you to be different and rightly so.

There was a time when my name was synonymous with the word unreliable. It was the running "joke" that I would show up late for appointments and meetings.

It wasn't that I didn't want to be on time. It's just that I was delusional when it came to my time management.

If I had to be somewhere at a given time, I would act as if I had all the time in the world to get where I had to go. I simply didn't do the math correctly.

When that happens, watch out. Get out of my way. I'm like a speed demon on the road, blaming other drivers, calling them slugs because they are not driving fast enough.

It never fails that these are the times that "Uncle Murphy" shows up and reminds me of one of his sayings: "Whatever can go wrong, will go wrong." Traffic chooses to come to a standstill.

Needless to say, I would show up late for my appointment and my first excuse was that the traffic was heavy. It wasn't a lie. It's all relative. Heavy traffic is more a perception than a reality at these times.

This pattern of mine became so predictable that those who knew me would expect this behavior from me.

One of my leaders would say to me: "Kingsley, I expect you to be late so, when you are, I'm not disappointed."

Whoa!

What she was saying was that I had become unreliable.

In the beginning, I would make light of her words and took it as a friendly jab. There were no serious consequences for my tardiness, so it continued.

Over time, it began to bother me until one day it hit home for me.

As I thought more about it, I eventually made a decision to change. I didn't like to be seen as unreliable.

I cannot remember how I came across the following paradigm of what it means when someone shows up late to appointments, but it was what turned things around for me.

"When you showed up late for an appointment, you're simply saying your time is more important than others. They can wait but you shouldn't."

Boom!

Hearing that was like someone punched me in the gut and knocked the wind out of me. I made a decision to change right then and there.

I was going to reverse the belief that I had created about showing up on time. I wanted to be dependable, be someone that could be trusted by showing up when I said I would.

Have I been late to an appointment since then? Yes, but I can assure you it's now the exception and not the norm.

If you have found yourself in a similar situation where your reputation followed or preceded you, make every effort to reverse that. If you don't, be assured you'll see the results in how they relate to you. You will not be trusted. You will be taken for granted. This will take the "wind" out of your leadership sail.

USE THEIR NAME OFTEN

People like to hear their names being used in positive conversations. Notice I said, positive conversations and not negative ones.

Unfortunately, what they often hear is their name being used in the latter, when something is wrong or when they do something wrong.

You want to change that dynamic. You want to be the leader who people love and want to follow. This is one way to do it.

First thing is to make sure you know people by name and, the second thing, use it often.

How often have I heard the excuse being used, "I'm not good with names." I must admit that I've been guilty of that. To change that, I had to admit to myself that I was acting lazily.

The message being sent is that your name is not important enough for me to take the time to memorize it. People, hear that message. They may not say anything about it, but don't think for a moment that they're not thinking that.

Here's what you'll do: use their name often when talking to them. Don't overdo it. Three times within a lengthy conversation is good enough.

You may want to learn the simple trick of name association. What this means is to find some way of associating their name with an object. It could be as simple as a facial feature. Once you have settled on what you'll use, attach that to their name.

For example, my name is Kingsley. I'm from Jamaica. If you knew that the capital of Jamaica is Kingston, you can associate my name with Kingston. Secondly, I have an accent. You could put it all together by saying, "Kingsley with the accent from Kingston, Jamaica."

The next time you see me and hear my accent, your brain will quickly scan your memory bank and retrieve the words accent, Kingston and Jamaica. Now, you'll remember my name.

It may be a bit challenging at first to make associations, but the more you practice, the better you'll become. But you'll only practice, if you see the importance of knowing someone's name and using it quite often.

MANAGE THEIR EMOTIONS

You might be wondering like I did when I first came across this idea of "managing the emotions of others." My immediate thought was, "how?" followed up by "is it possible?"

I understand the idea of managing my own emotions. That I get. But managing someone else's emotions should be up to them. That is their responsibility.

These were some of my thoughts until I learned what it meant to be emotionally intelligent and hence become an Emotelligent Leader.

Relationship Management is one of the four quadrants used to define emotional intelligence. It is the ability to use awareness of your emotions and the others' emotions to manage interactions successfully.

What this simply means is you become sensitive to the emotions of others.

One of the immediate push-backs I receive from some leaders is that they are not the sensitive type. This is more so from male leaders.

When they hear the word emotional used in any sentence, they are hearing that they are being asked to be soft and for some, to be weak. They associate softness and weakness with the word emotional.

I get that because I grew up hearing something similar. That association was ingrained within me.

Until …

… Until I found out the fallacy of that thinking.

Being sensitive to others is an indication of how well adjusted you are in managing your own emotions. You are not going to be able to identify other people's emotions if you don't know what it "looks" like. It takes one to know one.

As an Emotelligent Leader in the making, you ought to be at least a fairly good judge of the emotions being communicated through one's body language as well as tone of voice.

Imagine seeing or hearing one of your team members look or speak as if something is wrong.

Because you've taken the time to "know" them, you become immediately aware of this. You know them enough to recognize something is off-kilter.

Having memorized that person's name and knowing this much about them, you do what most leaders don't ... take time to ask -- to be curious.

Framing the conversation in what you've seen or heard, contrasting it with what you know of them will increase your standing with them. You have sent a strong message to everyone ... they matter.

The more you are able to do this, the more you strengthen your social awareness skills. The more you are able to strengthen your social awareness skills, the better positioned you will be to manage the relationships around you.

TAKEAWAYS

Leadership is Relationship :_____

_____

_____

_____

_____

_____

CHAPTER 12

LEADERSHIP IS PARTNERSHIP

There's an African proverb that says, "If you want to go fast, go by yourself. If you want to go far, go with others."

One of my favorite writers is Solomon who wrote: "… one standing alone can be attacked and defeated, but two can stand back-to-back and conquer; three is even better, for a triple-braided cord is not easily broken."

Both the words of the African proverb and those of Solomon suggest that having a partner to do life with is important. It gives you an advantage in certain situations.

In this context of leadership, you might wonder if that is necessary. Why would you as a leader need to concern yourself about partnering with anyone when you are the "boss." You are the one in charge. Why should you partner with those you are leading to get the job done? Why shouldn't they simply follow your directives and do what's asked of them?

This is one of the mistakes leaders who fail, make. They think they can go the distance by themselves. It's an ego thing for some. For others, it's an insecurity issue. And, still, for others it's not something they've ever even considered ... partnering with those they lead.

I used to be that guy. I had all the issues stated above. I'm so glad I came to my senses quickly enough before I ruined everything and joined the ranks of those who failed in leading others.

I had an independent mindset. I grew up hearing this phrase: if you want to get something done the way you want it done, you've gotta do it yourself. Did you hear that as well?

A part of me felt that if I asked for help or partnered with others, it was a sign of weakness and incompetence. With this in mind, I pushed myself to be superman. I rarely said no. If it could be done, I was the guy to get it done.

What I found out was that I craved attention. I wanted the applause of my peers and more importantly, my bosses. I wanted to hear my name being mentioned in meetings alongside the accomplishments. I soaked it up without taking the time to give credit to those who, in some way, helped me to accomplish the tasks.

So, I understand if you too are having a hard time seeing partnership as beneficial to leadership.

When you lead as a partner, those you are leading to accomplish certain tasks are open to:

- Collaboration

- Better communication

- An increase in knowledge

- Accountability

- Building trust

- The efficient use of resources

Let's take a look at how this is made possible.

COLLABORATION

We are living in a time when we are more and more dependent on others. No one of us will be able to master every skill necessary to get the job done, especially in this information age.

There's so much information to navigate. Not only that, we also have such explosions taking place in the technological world. I don't know about you, but it makes my head spin when so much is coming at me. Social Media. Smart phones. Smart TVs. Personal Assistant Devices. It's very hard to keep up. You would need a full-time job just to learn and manage them all.

That's why collaboration is so key to our overall success.

As a leader, your winning strategy should be to surround yourself with others who will help you "keep up." You don't have to be a know-it-all or stress yourself over not knowing about every single thing. You can't.

It was the late Henry Ford who was demonized for not being qualified for the position he held as CEO of the Ford Motor Company.

The accusation was that he didn't know much. When asked certain questions about the company and its operation, he would have to ask one of his direct report executives.

After having had enough of these accusations that were meant to embarrass him, he decided to respond to his "tormentors."

His response went something like this: "Why should I spend my energy and time trying to know everything about the manufacturing industry when all I need to do is pick up the phone and make a call and get the answer I need? "

Henry Ford realized the importance of having capable people around him to get the job done.

You and I need to do the same.

Not only do we need to surround ourselves with people who are capable of assisting in running the organization, but we need to have people who are more knowledgeable in areas we are not, so that together we can get the job done...better.

I remember hearing this phrase: "Two heads are better than one." Another phrase I grew up hearing is that, "Many hands make light work." These sayings are so true.

Solomon said it like this, "two are better than one. If one falls the other can pick him up."

What all this means, in essence, is, "it is easier for two people, who help each other, to solve a problem than it is for one person to solve alone."

To be successful at collaborating, it requires you to put aside one of the most difficult ego-driven qualities for many leaders ... PRIDE. This is so hard for some. They would rather "die" than show that they don't have it all together or know all things.

That was me.

As I discussed earlier, my pride tripped me up many times. I had so many unfinished projects and took on so many tasks because my pride demanded I do so. I was a slave to my pride.

How much easier would it be if I only adhered to the words of Solomon: "Two are better than one" and the age-old maxim "two heads are better than one."

I can attest to the fact that when I reached out for help and, according to the late Bob Marley, "emancipated myself from mental slavery," I freed my mind.

Collaboration gives true meaning to teamwork. And, as cliché as it may sound, "Teamwork truly makes the dream work."

BETTER COMMUNICATION

It's almost impossible to partner with others for any length of time and not learn how to better communicate with them.

You quickly learn that not everyone communicates the same way.

Some people like detailed-style communication, whereas others like summarized-style. You will be better positioned to detect the different styles of communication among your team, the more time you spend with them.

You will discover this one secret: communication is more than just words.

The many studies done on communication state that nonverbals--body language--accounts for about 80 percent or more of communication.

Being able to manage your emotions and communicate them through your body language in a way that is inviting, warm, and confident is a winning trifecta.

You are always communicating something to your team. They are always picking up cues directly or indirectly from your nonverbals.

If you don't believe me, try coming to the workplace or wherever you gather with your people having a bad attitude, and see what happens.

It's not long before they get the message from your mood and quickly determine how to "dance" around you for the remainder of the day or until your mood changes.

What you'll notice is similar to what you see at night when you turn on the lights in your kitchen and roaches scatter. As soon as the light goes on, you'll see roaches scattering as fast as they can to somewhere they can "hide."

That's how your team behaves when they see you coming toward them with what they perceive as a bad attitude. They scatter.

When you are able to manage your emotions and learn to become a better listener, you'll find yourself working hard at adjusting your communication style to your team.

The key to this is become a better listener.

Great communicators are great listeners.

You will need to get past just hearing what is being said to you and move to listening to what's being said.

This requires focused attention. You are required to use more than your ear to listen. The need to make good eye contact is paramount to effective listening.

The person you are listening to must know that he or she is the most important person to you at that time.

Being on your phone, looking past or away from the person you are speaking with, appearing to be occupied doing anything else than being focused on your "target audience" is indicative of you not fully listening.

The argument that some of us make is that we are able to listen and do other things at the same time. In other words, we are able to multi-task. We brag about how well we can do this.

For your information, though, research argues against the human's ability to multi-task. In fact, MIT Professor of Neuroscience Earl Miller, says when you attempt to multi-task, the brain is forced to switch among multiple cognitive tasks and this sort of task-switching is very unproductive.

So, even if your brain were effectively able to do so, it is simply not good manners. The message being sent is that what you are doing is equally important and sometimes more important than the person in front of you.

If, and when, your team member thinks that you are not listening to them, they'll simply stop coming to you. You will miss out on possibly very important information.

Not only that, according to Andy Stanley, "leaders who refuse to listen will eventually be surrounded by people who have nothing significant to say."

Making your "listener" feel as if he or she is the most important person at the moment will elevate you in their eyes. You will become the leader who is loved and cheerfully followed.

This is the power of listening and becoming a better communicator. The better you become at communicating, the more you will attract people to want to be around you.

INCREASE YOUR KNOWLEDGE

None of us know everything. Like me, you may feel like you do and that how you do things is perfect; no one can do it as good as you. That was the past version of me.

It was hard for me to ask for help.

As stated earlier, asking for help was a sign of weakness for me and an admission that I wasn't as smart as I projected myself as being.

This mindset led to a lack in some areas of my life. I had created a no-growth environment for myself and didn't even know it.

In my small circle, I seemed to be the smartest one because I was almost always being sought out for my "wisdom."

Granted, many people did attest to the fact that I was helpful to them and that's why they came back and sent others my way.

Yet, this only fed my ego and created a trap for me.

How can I now seek out knowledge from others with my reputation as Mr. Know-It-All? It would certainly "ruin" my reputation.

Thankfully, I came to my senses quickly and realized how dumb my thinking was.

If I had stopped for a moment to think it through, I would have looked around me and saw that I was where I was because of knowledge I gained through life experiences and, most importantly, through learning from others.

When you "partner" with others and enter that partnership with an open mind, you will be better off at the end of the day.

Here's what you are saying when you decide to take time to partner with your team. You're, in essence, telling them that you trust what they bring to the table. You are elevating their status to one of importance.

When they see that, they are more inclined to want to share as much as they know with you.

This has happened to me countless times, both with my children and the people I've led throughout the years.

My children know more about trends than I do. When I let go of my pride and am willing to seek their wisdom in areas in which I am a novice, it's amazing how much and how willing they are to share with me what they know.

I've learned so much from them and still do.

This is also true within the workplace.

I've had some very capable and smart leaders who I've had the privilege of overseeing. Many of them were geniuses to me when it comes to the tasks I had delegated to them.

Learning to be curious and asking lots of questions helped me become more knowledgeable on topics I was clueless about.

Here's the key: everyone has something to teach us.

We can always learn even if it is how not to do or say something. It's still learning.

Remember, you have access to a collective reservoir of knowledge. Make good use of it. You and your organization will be better as a result of you partnering with your team, an important part of your leadership journey.

The success I had in one of my leadership positions wasn't because I was an exceptional leader, it was because I was a smart leader willing to lead through people who were better in areas than I was. The same will be true of you.

GENERATE IDEAS

Not only does partnering with your team help with communication and increase in knowledge, it also helps with generating more ideas than if you were to do the work all by yourself.

Imagine what would happen if you took your experience, wisdom and knowledge and combined that with another person who has their own experience, wisdom, and knowledge?

If there are two things that I know, it would 1) make tasks more manageable and 2) allow for the contribution of ideas you could never have generated on your own.

How many times have I had an experience where my original idea was replaced with a new way of looking at the problem after having other people share their perspectives and insights on the issue. It's too many times to mention.

Abraham Maslow said, "I suppose it is tempting, if the only tool you have is a hammer, to treat everything as if it were a nail."

You and I are limited to the set of tools we have in our tool chest. This limitation will lead to us more than likely coming to the same conclusion over and over again. We only have a hammer.

However, if another person or other persons were to bring their tools and combine them with ours, we now have a cache of tools we never had before. It makes the job easier when we have more tools available to us.

I remember one day trying to replace the brakes on my car. Yes, there was a time when I did some of my own minor mechanical repairs, which included changing brake pads.

In the process of changing the pads, I encountered a problem. One of the nuts would not budge no matter what I tried. It was a hot day, so the more I tried, the hotter I became and the more frustrated I got.

My brother-in-law who is a mechanic had some tools that I didn't have, which would have made the task so much easier. He had air-powered tools.

I sat there and imagined the sound of his air-powered tool whirring as it effortlessly removed the nut.

After a few seconds of imagination, I picked up the phone and called him.

I was so happy to hear that he was home. I asked if I could come over and borrow his tool to remove the nut.

He said yes, for which I was thankful.

I put the parts I had removed back in place and drove over to his house. He lived a few miles away, which made it even better.

Upon arriving at his house and explaining to him what was happening, I then listened to his expert suggestion as to the approach I should take and what tool would be best to use. We then went to work.

We hoisted the car with the jack and, within minutes, we had that nut pulled and were able to replace the brake pads in no time.

I could have kicked myself for not thinking about this earlier. But it was my ego and pride at play.

134 | KINGSLEY GRANT

As you read on, you will see me confessing, at different places, how my pride and ego got in the way of my leadership and why.

Here's one thing I know: I like a good challenge. Being able to take on a challenge and overcome it makes me feel powerful. Unfortunately, this wasn't true for me with replacing the brakes. This job had me beaten. I felt powerless.

I learned quickly the lesson of "two is better than one" and that Leadership is indeed Partnership.

TAKEAWAYS

Leadership is Partnership: _____

_____

_____

_____

_____

_____

_____

CHAPTER 13

LEADERSHIP IS MENTORSHIP

Two quotes that I've used within my leadership training that I believe captures the idea of mentorship are from leadership guru John Maxwell.

The first one is: "Leaders must be close enough to relate to others, but far enough ahead to motivate them." The second one: "A leader is one who knows the way, goes the way, and shows the way."

This falls in line with one of the many definitions of mentorship found online. The one that resonates mostly with me is the one below.

Mentorship is a relationship in which a more experienced or more knowledgeable person helps to guide a less experienced or less knowledgeable person. The mentor may be older or younger than the person being mentored, but he or she must have a certain area of expertise.

Do you have a mentor or someone you would consider to be a mentor to you?

Unfortunately, I cannot answer in the affirmative that I have a mentor but there are people in my life, both past and present, that I view as mentors. Some of these people I have never physically met but I view them as mentors because of the influence they've had on my life through their writings and other forms of presentation.

I grew up being quite prideful. I don't know where I got it from but it was hard for me to ask for help. I had a "know-it-all" attitude. Asking for help seemed like a form of weakness. It suggested that I didn't know something, and I couldn't "afford" that.

I wanted to appear strong. Knowledgeable. Competent. Smart. All of that was a cover for pride.

Having someone who would "take me under their wing" and show me the "ropes" wasn't for me. "Who could ever teach me anything?" I thought.

Another dilemma was that it required me to get close to someone and share my "space" with them. That was too close for comfort. I didn't want anyone to find out the truth that I really didn't know what they thought I did. A mentor would.

When it came to mentoring others, I had no problem with that as long as I could do it from a distance. I didn't have the "time" for "close" mentoring. I was busy or acted busy.

I did offer suggestions, advice, and counsel to many. But it was all done from a distance.

Thank God that all that changed when I truly became a leader.

Having studied the life of Jesus, who to me is the greatest leader ever to walk this earth, I began to realize what true leadership was.

One of the authors of the scriptures, John, wrote: The Word (Jesus) became flesh and blood, and moved into the neighborhood. This is quoted from the Message Version of the Bible.

The picture that is conjured up in my mind is that of a celebrity type person who goes into a poor neighborhood, rolls up his or her sleeves, and helps in whatever way he or she can to relieve some of the hardship of the people living there.

Whether it be holding sick children, bathing them, feeding them or finding other ways to make the lives of those people better.

Even though some do it for the cameras, many do it out of genuine care.

That's the picture I have in mind when I think of leadership as mentorship.

It's not necessarily that you do the above, but it's the idea of getting in close proximity to those you are leading and mingling with them.

When they are able to see and feel that you are "with" them, they are more open to giving you "permission" to mentor them. They are more willing to allow you to give them some of what you have. You have made yourself attractive to them. They want to follow you.

So how do you go about mentoring someone who has been "won" over by your actions and see you as a possible mentor?

There are four major parts to this.

138 | KINGSLEY GRANT

The first is "show them."

SHOW THEM

You begin showing them by letting them watch you do what you do. One of the terms used is "shadow you." Another is to let them "look over your shoulder."

There are many industries that use this method to train new employees.

The new hire will be assigned to a veteran for several days. The veteran will explain to the new hire what he or she is doing and why.

One of the pitfalls I find with this method is that the new hire is expected to remember everything they were shown and told. The reality is they forget almost everything.

Secondly, if the mentor isn't onboard with the company and its vision/mission, he or she will deliberately hold back important information from the new hire. They will give them the bare minimum, making the argument that they're not being paid enough for the task.

As someone who is becoming the leader everyone loves and cheerfully follows, you have to first make sure you are on board with the vision and mission of the organization. Your heart must be in it.

Once you've settled that, you deliver all you know to the person you are mentoring. Show and tell them everything they need to know. Hold nothing back. You want them to be successful.

One of the late Zig Ziglar's favorite quotes is "You can have everything in life you want, if you will just help other people get what they want."

How true this statement is. You will be the beneficiary if you take the time to mentor properly.

Imagine the person you have mentored becoming as good or better than you are and is able to do what you do. Then, imagine a new opportunity arises whether in the organization or somewhere else taking on a new business venture; you are now able to do it because you don't have to worry about leaving.

You might be where you are and remain where you are not because other opportunities aren't available, but simply because you cannot see how you could leave your "post."

But, also imagine not mentoring as you ought to have done and something happens where you have to leave and the person you were mentoring stepped in to take over, either temporarily or permanently. How would you feel about him or her at the "helm" while you were not there?

I heard a story of an old carpenter who was going to retire from building homes. He wanted to spend the rest of his life, while retired, traveling with his wife and doing things he had always wanted to do.

One day he shared his plans with his boss - the man he worked for and built most of his homes.

His boss was sad to see him go because he was one of his best employees whose work was to be admired. He - the boss - wanted to do something special for him but wanted it to be a surprise.

He asked the carpenter to do him one last favor ... build him one more house.

The carpenter reluctantly agreed, seeing that this was it and he could use the extra money.

He began the project but his heart wasn't fully in it. He also saw it as an opportunity to cut some corners, save some money, and pocket the difference. His boss would never know.

The carpenter bought cheaper materials, used refurbished items, and sometimes, used old leftover scraps in places that would not be seen.

The day finally arrived when the house was completed. Looking at the house, one could not tell he had done such a shabby job.

His boss came by and examined the house and was very pleased with what he saw. Little did he know what his trusted employee - the retiring carpenter - had done.

After walking through the house, going from room to room, nodding his head with delight, and smiling with the carpenter as they both walked throughout the house, he did something totally unexpected.

He shook the hand of the carpenter and thanked him for such a splendid job and for agreeing to do him this one last favor and then handed him the keys to the house.

He said, "This is my gift to you. You have been a very good employee and I could not think of a better way to say thanks to you. Welcome to your new home."

The carpenter was in shock. He didn't know what to say. It wasn't so much because of the gift in and of itself. It was the fact that he had cut many corners and used the cheapest materials he could find including refurbished parts in building the house.

Had he known that the house would have been his, he would have spared nothing. He would have used the best of the best — so it is with mentoring.

If you knew the person you are mentoring would be called upon to relieve you of your "post" so that you could be free to advance yourself and that you would need someone in this position that would be as good as you or better, how would you mentor them?

Would you hold anything back from them? I don't think so.

That's the spirit of mentoring that we as leaders need to have. They will be more open to us going to the next step.

DO IT WITH THEM

The second stage of mentoring is for the mentee to do what it is you've taught them, alongside you.

I remember my dad teaching me to drive. I was about twelve or thirteen years of age at the time.

Not being old enough or tall enough to reach the pedals or be behind the wheel by myself, my dad had me sit in his lap while I changed the gears and steered the vehicle.

I had watched him drive hundreds of times and, at times, he would tell me what he was doing, especially when changing the gears. His vehicles had manual shifts so the timing of the shift had to be just right. You had to listen to the engine and use that as a guide.

Now, it was my turn to do it with him right there "beside" me.

He would tell me when to shift the gears while he depressed the clutch. I began to learn to listen to the engine and knew when it was time to make the shift.

He was doing it with me.

I felt safe. He was within sight and reach. I didn't have to panic if something happened that I might not have been able to handle.

This helped me to build my confidence as I had one small win after another. Each time I had an opportunity to "drive," it became a win.

What my dad had to do was exercise great patience with me. If he saw that I had shifted in the wrong gear, he would keep depressing the clutch while I did a "take-two" and corrected it.

If I failed to put on the indicator when making a turn, he would gently remind me. I must say that he did lose his patience with me from time to time when I kept on making the same mistake over and over.

In those moments, I felt a bit rattled and not as confident, wondering if I would ever be able to get it right. He would help me to "shake it off" and move on.

As I grew taller, became older, and was now able to reach the pedals, my dad felt it was time for me to get behind the wheel while he sat in the passenger seat. He was now ready to watch me drive.

Like my dad, "doing it with them" will require much patience. Above all, it will require you to manage your emotions.

This is a critical time for your mentee. It's a make or break time.

It's easy to have your words and body language taken out of context or be misinterpreted. There is a heightened sensitivity to one's confidence at this time.

If my dad "lost it" because I wasn't catching on quick enough and used words such as stupid or dumb to describe what I was doing or did, what do you think I would hear? If you said I would hear that I'm stupid or I'm dumb, you're right.

Even though my dad may have been referencing what I was doing, I more than likely would not have heard that.

The point is to be very mindful that this period of "doing it with them" is a delicate time and requires you to be self-aware, managing your emotions and the emotions of your mentee.

Now it's time to promote them and watch them at "work."

WATCH THEM DO IT

Under my dad's watchful eye and having had the practice, it was time for me to get behind the wheel of the car.

Knowing that I was now in control of starting the car, depressing the pedals, shifting the gears, and steering a moving vehicle, it felt a little overwhelming. I had quite a bit of butterflies floating around in the pit of my stomach.

However, knowing that I had done it with my dad so many times, I felt courageous. Being courageous doesn't mean the absence of feeling fear, but it's doing it anyway while having the fear.

Even though getting the car in motion wasn't as smooth as when my dad did it, I was able to get the car moving.

I got better the more I did it, learning from the mistakes I made and listening to my dad - the expert - as he pointed out what I could do better and what I did well.

To say that my dad didn't raise his voice and, at times, had me pull over and take over the driving, would be dishonest.

However, he and I were determined that I was going to learn to get it right and I did…over time.

He watched me do it until it was time to let me do it on my own.

This is what you will have to do with those you are mentoring.

Like my dad, there will be the temptation to take control and get behind the "wheel" yourself. It seems easier and with less hassle.

At times you will be watching from the "sidelines" with fear and trembling because you're seeing the "accident" about to happen.

There are times I saw my dad pressing hard on the floor of the passenger side where he was seated, mimicking pressing the brakes.

Other times, he moved his body even though slightly, in the direction of where he think I should be turning the car.

The success came from him resisting the temptation to take control even though he did on occasions.

To "watch them do it" requires patience, self-control, and perseverance. You must also trust that what you've taught will take effect. Having the confidence in your mentee will make them more confident, which will expedite the process of learning.

Having frequent feedback sessions is helpful to hear what your mentee might still be struggling with and for you to offer some suggestions as to how they could improve.

Finally, it's time for "graduation."

LET THEM DO IT

This is D-Day!

My dad had built up enough confidence in my driving. Having watched me do it for some time, he felt comfortable enough to let me drive the car without him being inside the car.

I know it wasn't easy for him to "release" me into the "wild," but he knew it was necessary for me to really feel what it was like to feel like I'm now a driver. Yay!

It felt great. I felt like I owed my dad to prove to him that his mentoring had paid off.

Driving as carefully as I possibly could became a high priority for me. I wanted to see his big smile as I returned home. Putting that picture in my mind helped tremendously.

My dad may have been nervous himself or maybe he wasn't. If he was, he hid it well, which helped me. If he showed any lack of confidence in me, it would have definitely added one more layer of nervousness. He managed his and my emotions successfully.

Like my dad, you too will have to practice maintaining your composure. Yes, it might be nerve-wracking and a nail-biting moment as your mentee gets "behind the wheel" by him or herself but do everything in your power to manage your emotions.

Put your facial muscles to work on your behalf as you display the biggest smile of confidence in the presence of your mentee.

What you do outside his or her presence is up to you. Run to the bathroom if you must or take some deep breaths. But do so after they leave your presence.

Like me wanting to make my dad proud, they will want to do the same for you. They are going to be a "little you" until they boost their confidence and develop their own style and rhythm.

But, whatever you do, let them do it by themselves. By doing so, they will one day develop enough expertise and confidence in themselves to want to be a mentor to someone else.

When they do that, they are in a sense, becoming an extension of you. How cool is that?

TAKEAWAYS

Leadership is Mentorship: _____

_____

_____

_____

_____

_____

CHAPTER 14

LEADERSHIP IS CRAFTSMANSHIP

John Maxwell in his book: "The 21 Laws of Leadership" identifies one of those laws as the "Law of the Lid."

He explains that this law helps people understand the value of leadership. The height of the lid determines a leader's level of effectiveness.

The lower the lid, the lower the potential is of your ability to lead. The higher the lid, the higher the potential of your ability to lead successfully.

To give you an example, if your leadership lid is an 8, then your effectiveness can never be greater than a 7. If your leadership lid is only a 4, then your effectiveness will be no higher than a 3. Your leadership ability—for better or for worse—always determines your effectiveness and the potential impact of your organization.

Some leaders fail to realize that leadership is more than a title and a position. These leaders became leaders because of time on the job, being the first in line for promotion based on tenure.

Because of this, leadership is not seen as a skill, but as a reward.

When you fail to see leadership this way, there's no attempt to further this skill or make it better.

It's only when you view leadership as a skill to be developed will you see the need to prioritize leadership development. Leadership is a craft. It is something that you develop and continue to develop.

The quote attributed to Abraham Lincoln: If I had eight hours to cut down a tree, I would spend the first six hours sharpening the axe" is very applicable in this chapter on the Emotelligent Leader.

To become better at anything, it requires practice. No one who is at the top of their game in any field has gotten there by simply having a title assigned to them.

One of the greatest athletes of all times is Jamaican sprinter Usain Bolt. It is without question that he was one of the most intimidating figures at the starting line in the 100 and 200-meter sprints. The records are there to prove it.

However, Usain Bolt didn't become the person that he is because of the admiration and cheers of his fans around the world.

Usain became the athlete he is from hours and hours of training. That was his way of "sharpening his tool."

Not only is this true of Usain in the track and field arena, it is also true of Michael Jordan who undoubtedly is one of the greatest basketball players of all times.

He too did not get this label because of someone's generosity. He worked for it. A quick Google search will give you some of the facts on his discipline in improving his game ... sharpening his axe.

One of the most common returns on my search that I came across was that he would practice an average of six hours a day shooting, dribbling and dunking the ball.

Imagine that many hours working on getting better at a craft. What would your leadership look like if you were able to give that much time to developing yourself as a leader? One thing I know is that you would be a much better leader than you probably are now.

In an article written by Forbes contributor Susan Kalla, entitled "Keys to Excellence (Even Michael Jordan Had to Do It)" she quoted Dr. K. Anders Ericsson, a Swedish psychologist, who says "deliberate practice, not inherited talent, determines success."

She continues by saying, "the practice must be long, sustained and ultra-vigorous. Standout athletes and professional business people commit to a minimum of 10,000 hours of focused practice to excel."

Having said all of that, it is important that you find a balance.

Why?

Some people may spend so much time "improving" that they never do any meaningful work. This is true of me from time to time. I get caught up in the "learning" phase, which keeps me from producing. I think at times I do so simply because it is easier and it soothes my conscience to not feel as guilty for not doing what I ought to be doing. It's hard to argue with learning.

As Abraham Lincoln states, it's six hours to sharpen the axe, but one must spend two hours working, which is to say — cutting the tree down. There comes a time that we must cut the tree down.

So how do you become better at your leadership craft?

It's called personal development.

PERSONAL DEVELOPMENT

A quote that is apropos to why it is important to develop your leadership craft is one by retired race car driver, Bobby Unser. He is known for saying, "Success is where preparation and opportunity meet."

I heard someone say that "growth today brings success tomorrow." If you want tomorrow to be better or more successful than today, you will have to do or learn something today that will make tomorrow different.

You may be familiar with the oft-used definition of insanity, which has been accredited to Albert Einstein. "The definition of insanity is doing the same thing over and over again but expecting different results."

So, if you are going to become better by developing your craft, you will need to concentrate on making your leadership skills better today than they were yesterday.

It's about learning from your mistakes, becoming more responsible, building your confidence, working smarter not harder, improving your communication and more.

This is called personal development.

Think of it as a muscle. The more you develop your muscles, the stronger they become.

I remember when I first started working out at a gym.

I had a friend who was in great shape. He had bulging muscles, ripped abs, and a look of confidence.

One day I mustered the nerve to ask him to help me achieve a physique that was anywhere in the ballpark of how he looked. If I were able to accomplish a fraction of his regimen, I would have been happy at that time.

He was very gracious to take some of his workout time to show me where to begin.

We began with weight lifting.

The cross bar alone weighed forty-five pounds.

He added a couple ten-pound weights on each side of the bar and, standing behind me, encouraged me to lift.

Knowing that he was right behind me with his hands resting on the bar, I took the challenge.

I took a deep breath as the experts do and pushed against the bar. I gave it everything I had, while straining to lift the bar.

With his help, I was able to lift the bar a couple times and then placed it back on the rack.

My arms felt like they were going to fall off.

We decided to give it a try another day. I needed to rest.

As we met for a few more weeks, I noticed something. My arms weren't as tired and he was adding more weights to the bar. I was becoming stronger.

Over time, I didn't need him as much anymore. My muscles developed in such a way that I felt comfortable enough to lift by myself.

So, it is in personal development.

It's a matter of consistency, repetition, and determination.

Like me wanting to develop my muscles, you too have to find what it is you want to develop.

Here's the catch: don't try to develop your weak areas.

Have you ever been told, or read, that you need to work hard at developing your weakness so you can be well-rounded?

I hope you didn't buy into that idea. Why would anyone want to spend their life working on their weakness, when they could be working on their strength?

There are areas in my life where I know I'm not as strong. I don't feel drawn to strengthening them. Nothing about that excites me.

Imagine telling someone like me to take the next year or more to work at seeing if I could fashion those weaknesses into strengths.

I might not be around at the end to know if it worked or not. It may have cost me my life.

If you tell me to work on my strength, you've got me. I'm excited about it. I would look forward each and every day to doing it.

What you want to do is to identify the areas that you are good at and seek to become better at those.

Communication is my strong point. Administration is not. Can you imagine having me spending time working on administration? I would attempt to do so, but I'd be pulling my hair out, which as it is, I don't have much of anyway.

Some of the ways you can do this is by reading books, listening to audio books and podcasts, attending workshop or conferences, or hiring a coach. These are just some suggestions.

On the topic of book reading-you probably know where I'm going with this, so brace yourself for it, "When was the last time you read a leadership book or leadership-related book?"

To repeat what leadership guru John Maxwell said in his book, The 21 Irrefutable Laws of Leadership, you will not be able to grow your organization beyond the level you are willing to grow yourself.

If ten is the maximum growth your company can attain and you - as a leader - are at a four or five, your organization will not grow beyond a three or a four. It cannot outgrow you.

Therefore, it is imperative for you as a leader to be intentional in growing yourself intellectually.

Reading leadership books is one way.

Another way would be attending leadership or leadership-related workshops and conferences.

Still another is to get involved in a mastermind group or having someone coach you in how to be better at leadership.

Napoleon Hill is quoted as saying, "No mind is complete by itself. It needs contact and association with other minds to grow and expand."

It's imperative that you seek out others who are within a similar space or industry as you do, and network/mastermind with them. You will be surprised what you'll learn and how having them as accountability partners can skyrocket your leadership abilities.

154 | KINGSLEY GRANT

I can personally attest to this, having been in different masterminds over the years, as well as leading my own. It's a game changer.

One of the great things about this is that you are surrounded by people of like-mindedness who may not be in the same space/industry as you, so they can bring fresh perspectives to the table. They are insiders who have outsiders' perspectives.

These are the best kinds of masterminds because there is no fear of competition but a sense of completion. Everyone wants the other person to complete what they started and become the best at what they do.

If you are focused on personal development, it tends to be contagious to the people you serve. They'll see you doing it and hear you talking about it ad nauseam that they'll want a piece of the action for themselves. Like begets likes.

Personal development is a must if you are going to become a better leader and raise your leadership lid.

ADVANCED LEARNING

This is one suggestion that only makes sense if where you are as a leader requires a more traditional form of learning.

Going back to a higher school of learning at this point in your life to become better at what you do may scare you. You probably would rather settle for the not-so-good-of-a-leader title than to think to commit to going back to school.

As I said, some contexts may require you to do so. If that is the case, plan to take on that challenge. You'll be glad you did. I am glad I did.

In 2004, I made a decision to return to college to pursue my master's degree. This was not an easy decision for me.

I was 47 years of age and it bothered me that at that stage of life, I was going to be competing with a much younger group of people who probably recently graduated from a 4-year college.

I felt embarrassed thinking about it.

It actually took me almost three years to make the decision. I was thankful to have had a very good friend who kept encouraging me to do so.

My decision was three-fold.

First, it was important to me to get my master's degree. It was fulfilling one of the goals I had for myself.

Secondly, it was to feed my ego. I would be the first in my family to have gone that far academically. I felt that it would give me an edge and also make my dad proud even though he had died many years prior. It's amazing how we can live our lives in the shadows of our parents and not even realize it.

Thirdly, it gave me more credibility to do some of what I'm doing today.

As an example: Who would you tend to believe or trust more, someone who had a degree and experience or someone who only had the experience but no degree?

For me, it's the former.

There's something about having that extra "piece of paper." It gets you into "doors" that a person without may not be able to get into. Mind you, this is not true in all cases.

As a leader, though, if the context in which you are leading makes it advantageous to pursue an advanced degree, I would say, go for it.

I was able to do it at an age that I thought I was too old, but I did it, graduating as a cum laude student within the top 3 percent of my class.

I gained skills that I'm using today in various areas of my professional life.

It was one more way of me sharpening my "tool" of leadership and it could be for you as well.

TAKE-AWAYS

Leadership is Craftsmanship :_____

_____

_____

_____

_____

_____

_____

CHAPTER 15

LEADERSHIP IS SALESMANSHIP

To think of leadership as salesmanship might be difficult for you. It seems to be that leadership and salesmanship are two different things all together and one should not have anything to do with the other.

That's what I initially thought myself.

When I think of the word salesman, it doesn't conjure up a positive image at the outset. Now it does, but initially it didn't.

Like myself, most people think of that sleazy used car salesman or that slick-willy door-to-door salesperson who try to use every conceivable method to separate you from your money. They'll stop at nothing even if they have to throw an in-law or two in the mix. The last part is for humor.

But you get the picture and may have at one point met that salesperson, as well.

So, to think of a leader who is someone who ought to be a person of high standard and integrity and to think of them being a salesperson, it seems like two contrary ideas.

I hope that after you've gone through this chapter, you'll have a different opinion of salesmanship.

One of my heroes in the inspirational world of speaking is the late Zig Ziglar. He often said this: "I have always said that everyone is in sales. Maybe you don't hold the title of salesperson, but if the business you are in requires you to deal with people, you, my friend, are in sales."

Zig believes that we all are in the business of sales. His thought is that we are all trying to sell something. In conversations, we are trying to sell our point of view. We want someone to believe, trust and maybe do what we say.

You, as a leader, are simply trying to get those you lead to buy into the vision, mission, and ideas of the company.

But it's how you go about doing it that makes all the difference.

You surely cannot be like the nefarious used car salesperson. You have to be more tactful and mindful of the overall welfare of the people you are leading as discussed in previous chapters. You have a whole lot more at stake.

To be successful at doing this, you'll need to be governed by your emotional intelligence.

As is true of any salesperson, so it will be for you when it comes to selling the vision, mission and ideas of the company.

One of the most important aspects of selling is that you need to believe in what it is you are selling.

I remember listening to one of Zig Ziglar's talks where he shared the story of a salesman who was selling appliances.

This salesman was having a difficult time selling the appliances and wanted some coaching from Zig as to how he could make more sales. At this stage, he simply needed to have at least one sale ... Period.

Zig talked about going to the salesman's home to understand more about what he was doing in his effort to sell the appliances.

After some time of talking, Zig noticed that this salesman didn't have any of the appliances he was selling.

He took it upon himself to ask this salesman why it is he didn't own any of the product he was selling.

The salesman gave him some weak answer as to why he didn't have that particular brand of appliance.

Zig immediately knew what the problem was. This salesman didn't believe in the product enough to purchase and use it for himself. Yet, he wanted to convince others of the need to purchase the product.

You, as a leader, must "purchase and use" the "product" - the vision, mission and ideas, of the company.

If you don't, you ought to do the ethical thing and step down from that position. Stop wearing the label of leader.

So how do you become a better salesperson as a leader? What does that look like?

Let's look through the lens of a salesperson to see what it is they do.

They educate.

THE EDUCATION

Salespeople have to educate their prospective customer on the benefits of the product they are selling. Notice I say benefits and not features. Selling focuses on benefits.

But if you are going to be successful as a leader-salesperson, you will have to focus on increasing your EQ.

The more Emotionally Intelligent you become, the more you are able to tap into the emotions of your people and "sell" them on your ideas.

Many leaders try to sell their people on facts and numbers. Booooring! To their people, it sounds like blah, blah, blah, blah, blah. Facts don't move people. It doesn't get to the emotions. People "buy" with their emotions and justify with their logic. Stories are what get people's attention.

Always remember this: Facts Tell. Stories Sell.

The better you are able to story your ideas, the better chance you'll have of getting your team to "buy."

In 1997, the Hay/McBer Research and Innovation Group, a large national insurance company, found that sales agents who were weak in emotional areas such as self-confidence, initiative, and empathy sold policies with an average premium of $54,000, while those strong in five of 8 emotional competencies sold policies on the average worth $114,000. Imagine that!

What we are able to learn from the above experiment is that salespeople who are low in EQ resort to selling without connecting to the universal human experiences and emotions. They are unaware of what people want so they try to sell them what they don't want. Facts. Features.

On the other hand, those with higher EQ are more self-aware, which makes them better at relationship management, so they are able to connect to the universal human experiences and emotions of their customers.

The salesperson with a lower EQ can become so enamored with their product and how it works and what it does that they forget that the prospective customer wants to know how the product will solve their most pressing issue - solve their problem ... ease their pain ... stop their "bleeding."

Most prospects don't care about your product. They only care about one thing — their pain.

When I have a headache and go to the pharmacy, I don't care initially about what the label is on the product, the color, or the ingredients. I simply want to know if that product is able to give me quick relief.

Don't get me wrong. I do look at the ingredients and so on, but not before I am sold on the idea that the product can give me the result I seek ... instant pain relief or as close to that as possible.

The promise is the benefit. It's answering the age-old question that all people want to know: "What's in it for me?" This is often referred to as WIIFM for short.

How does this apply to the people you are leading?

Your job is to educate them on the benefits of them doing their best work. That is the bottom line.

What are the benefits?

I would suggest finding a way to connect the vision/mission to their emotions. Find out what is it that you will be able to "sell" them that will bring them a sense of fulfillment, pride, and joy.

Remember, people "buy" first with their emotions and then justify it with their mind.

I'm not a shopper. My wife is.

She will go to the mall and spend hours upon hours and come home with no purchase. It would "kill" me to do that.

At times, she invites me to go with her just to get my reaction, and predictably, the answer is "It's okay honey, you go ahead."

For her, it's therapy, whereas, for me, its torture. I'm being a little bit overdramatic here, but you get the point.

However, if there is something I really want and I've researched where to get it, I'll go to that store, go straight to where that item is, purchase it, and I'm out of there.

If it can be done online, I'm in.

Here's the thing, because I'm not a "shopper," I'll see or hear something that catches my attention by evoking an emotion in me, and immediately my brain says, "you need that."

I'll move toward that thing and purchase it and then I'll sell my wife or whoever on why it was such a good buy.

Someone knew how to "hook" me.

What is your hook?

Your hook has to be based on how it will make their lives better: feel better or look better.

For example, you could sell them on how they will be the envy of their peers as a result of their hard work.

You could also sell them on the public recognition and rewards they will receive for a job well done. This could be a recognition in the monthly newsletter, at a special dinner, or general meeting.

Help them imagine themselves standing there being recognized in that manner.

The more you do this, the better you'll become as a salesperson. The better you become as a salesperson, the more productive your team will become.

SELLING TO THEM

Some organizations need to do a better job of putting together their vision statement. It makes it difficult for employees and others to keep it at the forefront of their minds.

There was a time that the in-thing was vision and mission statements. I remember helping the organization for which I spent a number of years working, crafting the mission and vision statement.

It was an interesting and time-consuming endeavor. The challenge was trying to say more by saying less and to make sure it was future-focused as all vision statements should be.

But the goal was to have it so tightly written that everyone would be able to memorize and repeat it without much effort. In addition, it was to help us all, especially those of us in leadership, make sure what we did and planned to do fit within the vision of the organization.

That is the ultimate goal of the vision statement.

If you as the leader aren't in full agreement with the vision of the organization, you will have a hard time trying to sell that to your team members. They will sense the incongruence within you.

There is an old adage that I grew up hearing, which is, "You can fool all the people some of the time and some of the people all the time, but you cannot fool all the people all the time." I have since learned that it is attributed to Abraham Lincoln. Oh well, I'll give it to him.

The vision is one thing you need to sell by finding creative ways to remind your people where the organization is headed and how they will be a part of it.

It's important that you let them know what's in it for them as we previously mentioned.

2. Sell The Mission

The difference between the mission and the vision statement is that the latter focuses on the future and serves as a source of inspiration and motivation.

An example that I think most people will remember, whether they were born at the time or not, is the vision laid out by one of the past presidents of the United States - John F. Kennedy.

He boldly proclaimed, while he was president, that in 10 years the United States would place a man on the moon.

At the time, he had no knowledge of how it would be done. One thing he was certain of was that the United States had the will, resources, and resourcefulness, to make it happen.

The vision was about the where. It inspired and motivated people as they rallied around this possibility. Within 10 years, the vision became a reality. The mission made it happen.

The mission is about how to do it. It focuses on the present. It answers the question of "What do we need to do to make it happen?" which is really a "HOW" question.

As a leader you need to be clear on the vision so that you can, together with your team, work out the "how" aspect of it. It becomes a collaborative or joint venture. In the chapter on

Leadership is Partnership, we discussed some of the value of collaboration.

In selling the mission, you are going to need a little more tact and skill to have your team "buy" from you.

This is where you are going to "roll up your sleeve" and do it with them.

I'm not suggesting that you do the work for them. No! But you are simply letting them know by your action, that you are very much in it with them.

Imagine being there with them, laughing, learning, working and playing - yes, I said playing, just in case you thought it was a typo.

You might not have a playful personality but you will have to learn to take moments to be uncomfortable so that your team will know that your message is loud and clear: "We win together or together we win." You choose.

I run the risk of being repetitive by once again reminding you that you have to link what you're doing with them as to how it's ultimately FOR them.

Your job is to show them how a win together means everyone wins. The organization wins and the team wins. You're willing to share the "spoils" with them. The "spoils" is the reward.

This is the art of selling as a leader.

You do this and you'll become the leader everyone loves and wants to follow. You will be an Emotelligent Leader.

TAKE-AWAYS

Leadership is Salesmanship: _____

_____

_____

_____

_____

_____

CHAPTER 16

LEADERSHIP IS DIRECTORSHIP

One of the most difficult challenges for a leader who wants to be loved and followed by all is making tough decisions. They are aware that these decisions could affect the relationships they have worked so hard to cultivate.

It's almost impossible to make tough decisions and make everyone happy.

As a dad, I want my children to love and follow my directives. This can be a balancing act since children don't have the capacity to process intellectually what seems like a contradiction: love and discipline. How can you love and discipline them at the same time?

However, as a dad, I know that because I love my children, I discipline them. In the book of Proverbs, Solomon states that a parent who doesn't discipline his/her child doesn't really love them.

As a leader, there comes a time when you have to "discipline" your "children."

This discipline could range anywhere from issuing a warning, putting someone on probation, and even firing them.

This is especially difficult if you became a leader through a promotion or because you were chosen by your peers to lead. You are placed in an awkward position to try and discipline or enforce policies and procedures.

There is almost an expected leniency when it comes to matters that require some form of discipline or correction. Some members expect VIP treatment. And if you dare step over the line to correct or discipline them, they are going to make sure you and others know about their disappointment.

You have to know how to separate the relationship from your leadership.

Leaders must be confident and secure enough to make tough decisions without making it personal. Having the right language and presentation makes a world of a difference.

You have heard the maxim: it's not what you say but how you say what you say, that matters!

There's a lot of truth in that. But I believe it's both and not one over the other. What you say - the words you use - is as important as how you say it - the tone you use.

Being a good communicator is one of the skills that Emotelligent Leaders develop. They are very aware of how to best make requests of others as well as issue directives.

Imagine that you want someone to sit in a certain chair. A person who has not been exposed to the Emotelligence paradigm might say in a commanding way: "Sit in that chair!"

They may get compliance or resistance in return. The former may come with an attitude whereas the latter could lead to a conflict of some kind.

An Emotelligent Leader, making a similar request, would say in a firm yet conversational way: "Would you please sit in that chair?" This approach is respectful, considerate, and humane.

This kind of request has a better chance of compliance and free of an attached attitude.

The problem with some leaders is that they are trying to force people to respect them. They use their title and position as leverage to get things done.

Is it any wonder that so many people on a team, in the workforce, or in other leadership settings, are giving their leaders such low marks?

Is it any wonder some who are able to leave an organization do so as soon as they get an opportunity? And some of these are the most talented of the group.

How then can you avoid some of the issues outlined above?

Begin with clarity.

GIVE CLEAR DIRECTIONS

Winston Churchill was known to be a no-nonsense kind of guy. He was very straightforward with what he had to say and wasn't as much concerned about who liked it or him in the process.

I'm not suggesting you emulate him, but I do admire his accomplishments and love this quote from him: "If you have an important point to make, don't try to be subtle or clever. Use a pile driver. Hit the point once. Then come back and hit it again. Then hit it a third time – a tremendous whack."

This, I believe, is one of the ways to minimize the drama that could ensue when corrective measures have to be implemented, which you will have to do at some point during your leadership.

Winston Churchill was also known to be a good communicator. He knew not only what to say, but how to say it.

Giving clear directions requires good communication.

Most leaders, if asked, would say they are very good communicators. They base this upon the "results" they are getting from what they say.

Yet these same leaders find themselves battling against those they are leading over meanings, misunderstandings, and misinterpretations of what was said.

How is that possible if directions were as clear as they assumed?

One of the phrases that I grew up hearing when someone thinks they gave clear directions is that their direction was as "clear as mud!"

A standing joke is that you should be careful when you receive "clear" directions from someone from the islands such as Jamaica - my country of birth.

If you have travelled to one of the West Indian Islands, which includes Jamaica, and have asked for directions, you may have had this experience.

When you are told "it's just around the corner," don't take it literally. It really doesn't mean it's around the corner. It maybe another half to three-quarters of a mile away.

This is also what you might hear as to how to get to your destination:

"Go down the street and when you get to the green house, take a right.

After you make the right, go further up the street and then once you get to the grocery store, make another right

and then at the big tree, make a left and

you'll then see the house you're looking for."

The person who gave you that set of directions is fully convinced that they have given you clear directions. In their mind, they are clearly seeing what they are telling you.

Maybe you are as confused as ever having just read the "clear" directions above.

The question is, was it clear?

Clear is relative. It's clear to the person who gave it but not so much to the person who heard it.

One of the most effective ways to know whether or not your directions were clear is to ask for feedback.

If people are doing things contrary to what you've asked them - the clear directions given - it is one of two things.

The first may be that they didn't fully understand what was stated.

The second may be that they are rebelling against what was said. They are being defiant.

What I've seen is that leaders mostly think the latter. And without checking to see if there could be another reason such as not fully understanding what was said, conclusions are drawn and the gauntlet is dropped.

This is how a non-Emotelligent Leader would react.

An Emotelligent leader, on the other hand, would first take responsibility for their part of the communication. They would make sure they revisited the conversation and compare "notes" to see where the breakdown occurred. Obviously, something did.

Once they've figured it out, they will make sure to improve on their part this time around.

Sometimes, they may not find any breakdown, but some other issues may surface, which they can address.

Regardless, clarification is necessary.

CLARIFY EXPECTATIONS

I'm not sure who coined the phrase, "It's not what you expect but what you inspect that gets done," but I've found it to be true on many occasions, both as an executive leader and as a parent leader.

This was never more so apparent than when we had leaders' meetings at one of my previous places of employment.

We would have leaders' meetings and spend hours and hours going over the agenda.

Not only was it frustrating at times to attend these meetings that seemed to have no end in sight, but to leave the meetings not knowing what the meeting was about or who was supposed to do what, was worse.

We discussed great plans and talked about these grandiose ideas, yet we would have these same discussions a week or weeks later.

If you were to ask the leader about whether or not they had communicated clear directions, they would promptly say, "Of course, don't you think so?" What am I going to say at those times, "No?"

So, what happened?

Why were we having these similar discussions a week or a few weeks later?

Here's why: a name wasn't assigned to the tasks.

What do I mean by that?

It's one thing to say, "We need to do this or that" and another to say "Sally is responsible for doing this or that."

Secondly, a time-table wasn't given. When should the task be completed?

There were expectations but nothing in place for inspections. Who do you ask about progress being made? How do you measure if it is indeed being made? What are the metrics?

It's hard to inspect something being done if we don't know who to hold responsible for getting it done and when it should be done.

Equally important is making sure that these expectations especially around policies, procedures, vision and mission are revisited often.

Don't simply expect that once these directions are given and clear expectations are outlined that they are going to always be followed up on. Most times they are not because erosion has taken place. Drifting occurs. People forget.

It's your responsibility to make it a habit to frequently go over your expectations especially when you notice drifting is occurring.

174 | KINGSLEY GRANT

As an adjunct professor at a local university, I'm asked by my department head to make sure I go over the syllabus with the students at the beginning of each cohort.

Most of these students have been through other classes where each professor is being asked to do the same thing.

It may seem repetitious and an over-kill.

At times, I observe the blank and disengaged looks on the students faces when it's time to go over the syllabus.

It's almost like they are saying, "We already know this!"

What I've found out is that, as the weeks go by, some students will do something that is forbidden by the syllabus. I will point it out to them and they will act as if this is news to them. And now, I have to take time to cite the page and paragraph that speaks to the particular issues.

Leaders who take the time to be clear on expectations and give clear directions are simply leaving nothing to assumption.

Someone has said that to assume makes an "ass-of-u-and-me." You don't want this definition to be true of you.

Being able to let people know who, what, where, how, and why, when it comes to expectations, will reduce most confusion and unnecessary conflict situation.

MODEL LOYALTY

It's important that as the leader you always do what's right for the company you lead. If at any point you cannot execute your duties because of a dispute or some irreconcilable differences between you and the company's policy or vision/mission, you should respectfully discontinue your leadership role.

The last thing you want to do is to undermine the company. It's very tempting to use this as an opportunity to make yourself look good and the company look bad. Emotelligent Leaders don't operate this way.

There is a scripture verse that has stayed with me since I was a child. It was drilled into me by my parents and others in both a right and wrong context. The verse says, "Whatsoever you sow, you shall also reap."

You never know when you'll find yourself in a situation where you would like for people who might not agree with you and are in conflict with you, to refrain from seeking to destroy you and your reputation.

You want them to do the mature thing and disagree but not be nasty about it.

Why would you want them to do that for you but you not want to do the same for the company you are serving?

I like the words of Jesus: "Do for others as you would have them do for you."

What you're doing is modeling integrity to those you are leading. You want them to also do like you do.

The Apostle Paul said to his mentee Timothy, "Follow me as I follow Christ." In other words, do as I do.

You as the leader must realize that you are influencing the lives of countless people. They are not only hearing what you say, they are watching what you do.

If you want to maintain a good "name" or reputation, you will need to do what's right before them as it pertains to matters like this.

Even when you are gone, they'll remember what you did. They'll talk about it. They'll use you as model of a leader they would want to follow. You become the "yardstick" by which they judge other leaders.

It was Charles Barkley, a basketball hall-of-famer, who once made this ridiculous statement in a commercial: "I'm not a role model. Just because I dunk a basketball doesn't mean I should raise your kids."

I agree with the latter part of the statement. Yes, no one should raise someone's kids but the parents of those kids.

However, he cannot abdicate the role assigned to him by many of his fans as a role-model. It goes with the territory. He failed to realize that he chose to be celebrated by showing his basketball skills, which other people want to emulate. If he didn't want that he should have chosen another career.

Some leaders are afraid to accept the fact that people look up to them. They are scared that they are going to let those people down. So, to avoid any confusion, they'll put the warning out ahead of time. They can point back to the fact that they had cautioned people from doing so. So, don't blame them.

This thinking is one that creates space for your disloyalty to those you serve. It weakens your leadership position. It creates confusion because team members won't know what to trust.

If you are not displaying a loyal attitude, they won't either. Why should they?

How do they know if you or the company are going to be around in the near future? It's hard to trust a person who is disloyal because you never know what they have up their sleeve.

When you show loyalty to your organization, you may not be liked, but you will be respected.

Be known for your loyalty.

And, remember, if the time comes when you can no longer be loyal, move on.

TAKING RESPONSIBILITY

You've probably heard the phrase, "The buck stops here." People who usually make that statement are those in a leadership position. They are simply saying that they are responsible for all final decisions.

However, some leaders will take credit for results that are positive but aren't so willing to take responsibility for the results when they are not as positive.

They will find someone or something to blame.

It's not their fault. They did their job. And they will try to find a scapegoat – someone on whom to pin the "tail of the donkey."

This has been an age-old technique that has plagued mankind.

From the very beginning of time, the very first man - Adam - tried this tactic of deflection.

God told him to not to eat of a certain tree in the garden where he lived. That tree was called the Tree of Life.

The story is told that his wife had ventured close to the tree one day and encountered the serpent, otherwise known as Satan.

Satan asked her, in a very sarcastic way, about the tree and what God had said.

Here's what he said: "Did God really say you must not eat of the fruit of any of the trees in the garden?"

She answered him by saying, "Of course we may eat fruit from the trees in the garden, it's only the fruit from the tree in the middle of the garden the we are not allowed to eat. God said, 'You must not eat it or even touch it; if you do, you will die.'"

He continued: "You shall not surely die. God knows that the day you eat it your eyes will be opened, and you will become like him, knowing both good and evil."

He finally persuaded her to try it and see for herself.

She foolishly picked the fruit and ate it, but also shared it with her husband Adam. For her to have done that, it meant he was close enough to watch the entire scene unfold. He never intervened and nothing is said about why he didn't.

After they had done that, God showed up and began to question them about what happened. He called a meeting with all the parties involved - Adam, Eve, and the serpent (Satan).

God posed the first question to Adam. "... Have you eaten from the tree whose fruit I commanded you not to eat?"

Adam replied, "It was the woman YOU gave me who gave me the fruit, and I ate it."

Adam was the leader. God had given him that position and role. And what do we find him doing? Deflecting! Blaming! Not taking responsibility! "It's not my fault!"

This is what some leaders do. But as it didn't go well for Adam, so it will be for leaders who do a similar thing.

To be an Emotelligent Leader who is loved by all and whom others want to follow, it requires that you take responsibility for the good, the bad, the ugly and all in-between.

To take responsibility especially when it's the bad and ugly requires a spirit of humility and vulnerability.

I see this a lot with losing teams when the coaches are being interviewed and being asked about the loss. I've often heard the good coaches take the blame for what happened. Very rarely do they "throw the team under the bus."

When you lead in this way, I guarantee you'll have a loyal team who will do their part to make things better. They will even make you look good when it wasn't your direct intent.

You'll become the leader they love and want to follow. They'll lay it on the line for you.

EVALUATIVE FEEDBACK

To evaluate something means to take a closer look at it, to judge, to scrutinize closely. These are just some of the phrases that could be used to describe what it means to inspect, as we discussed earlier.

As you read earlier about the need to be clear in what you expect from your team members, it is only half of the equation. Evaluative feedback is the second half.

One surefire way to destroy your working relationship with your team is to express disappointment in their work when you didn't provide feedback along the way.

If a team member performed unsatisfactorily over an extended period, why didn't they know that they were so off-course?

Is it because they were not told what was expected of them? Is it because they didn't hear what was said to them? I don't think so.

What generally happens is that the message you thought you communicated so clearly is not the message they heard. And because you didn't take the time to check-in with them to make sure that the message sent and the message heard were on par, both you and they were left to assume. They assumed they understood you, and you did likewise.

The result spoke for itself.

At one of the jobs I worked, I'll never forget how one of the staff members was fired and the rift it caused. I'm not sure if the individual ever got over the way she was fired.

I was not privy to all that went on. However, the account given by the terminated employee made it seemed as if she were fired without any warning. According to her, it came as a surprise. She never saw it coming.

The reason given for her firing was that she was not able to perform the work as expected. She fell behind and wasn't producing.

She argued that if she wasn't producing, why wasn't something said along the way. Why didn't she know this until it was too late?

Again, I wasn't privy to all that happened to know whether or not she had a genuine argument or if her firing was a legitimate one.

What I do know is that it's possible that her firing was a surprise.

Her boss wasn't the most organized person. He wasn't known to give clear directions or outlined expectations in a manner where a person knew what he or she was being asked to do. So, it's possible she had a valid point.

On the other hand, I knew that she had some personal challenges that interfered with her ability to do the work assigned to her.

Regardless of who was right, the outcome reflected a breakdown in the evaluation or feedback process. She shouldn't have been surprised or left with such a bad taste in her mouth. From what I know, it took years for her to come to terms with how the matter was handled.

This could be avoided if evaluative feedback was periodically done.

Giving evaluative feedback requires certain skills that some leaders simply don't have. It also requires timing. You must choose the right time and place to offer feedback, especially if it leans more on the negative side.

This is one of those not-so-fun jobs that you as the director of the "ship" has to do especially when you have a close relationship to the person with whom you are giving the feedback.

Setting boundaries and making it clear from the very beginning is crucial to how well this interaction goes.

Even though the promise of this book is that you'll become the leader everyone loves and wants to follow, giving honest evaluative feedback may create some tension and stress on relationships.

One way to minimize fallouts is to become skilled at your delivery.

In my leadership workshops, I teach the "sandwich method" of delivering effective evaluation.

What this means is that you deliver the feedback in a way that you will be thanked afterwards.

Imagine having a turkey sandwich with whole wheat bread or any bread of your choice. What you are looking at is a sandwich with the turkey meat on the inside of two slices of bread.

Label each side of the bread as praise and the meat inside as the feedback.

Start off by genuinely praising the team member by citing something positive about their work. It could be their diligence, patience, going above and beyond, and so on.

Having done that, you now transition into the meat of the evaluation sandwich.

Here is a caution: Do not use the word BUT.

The word BUT makes what was said before insignificant and irrelevant. What you are saying is that what comes after the BUT is more important. That is what people hear, even though you meant for them to hear what came before, as well. You may have found, in your own experience, that that doesn't work.

A good way of transitioning is to instead use the word AND. To make it more effective, you could follow up with a question.

Here's an example of what it would look like if I were giving you feedback. I'm going to give you the name Kirk. If your name is Kirk, simply play along.

Me: "Kirk, I wanted to follow up on the project you are working on. It is apparent that you are working very hard at completing it on time. I've heard that you go above and beyond at times to make sure you're doing your part. Thanks so much for that.

As we continue this project, I'm wondering how we could ensure that it stays on course as we had discussed at the beginning. I really want you to get it right. Do you have any suggestions?"

PAUSE.

Notice a few things I did.

I —

- Used his name
- Complimented him on some of his positive attributes
- Demonstrated the fact that I am engaged in the ongoing project by mentioning what I had heard about his work ethic
- Thanked him

Having done that, I'm now ready to deliver the meat of the sandwich. But notice what I did. I asked for his expertise, which is one more way of paying him a compliment.

I would then listen to his response and if it fits within the scope of what I had in mind, I would suggest we go ahead with his suggestion.

What do you think would happen?

Here's what I know Kirk would do. He would leave my office:

- Empowered
- Encouraged
- Upbeat
- As a "Fan"

On the other hand, if Kirk's suggestions were way off from what I had in mind, I would say something like this.

Me: "Kirk, your suggestions are good ones and I appreciate you sharing them. However, I'd like us to try something a bit different. Let's see how this would work."

I would then make my thoughts known and follow them up with, "Thanks for being willing to try what I'm suggesting and we'll circle back next week Monday at 4pm to see how things are rolling along. Can I count on you to give it your all?

I would wait for his response.

PAUSE.

Notice how I framed my suggestion. I first acknowledged his suggestions and my appreciation for them and then made my suggestion. I followed up with another "thank you" for being willing to try my suggestion. As you can see, I didn't give him an option.

Once he responded, I'd then close our meeting with the other slice of bread - the other praise.

Me: "Kirk, thanks for your hard work and dedication. Knowing this about you gives me great assurance that what we agreed on today will be executed with the same approach you bring to your work. Man, I really appreciate that. Thank you."

PAUSE.

Again, you'll notice my gratitude, acknowledgment of his work ethic and integrity, and giving him a specific time that we'll follow up to see how progress is being made.

This is a smooth interaction. I know there are more complicated ones, especially when dealing with a team member who, for whatever reason, hasn't bought fully into the vision and mission of the organization.

A person is better prepared to hear a critique that's done with acknowledgment of something they have done right.

Taking the time to highlight both the positive and the not-so-positive makes the feedback more palatable.

It's like giving a child, and even some adults, medication that is not the best tasting. They may gag on it and even vomit as a result of it. It's a fight with some children.

However, if you mix the medication with something tastier or hid it in something more desirous, they would probably not fight it as much. Sometimes they don't even know until you tell them.

That is how you want to give an evaluation.

The recipient, at times, doesn't even realize that you have given them "medication" that is not the most tasteful. They are aware of it, but it doesn't "taste" that way.

It's impossible to address every scenario here. What most business owners and leaders do is have me consult with them to work through their specific issues. This normally coincides with a leadership training workshop that I would do for them.

The most important thing to remember when leading through the lens of directorship is to make sure you see a person, as a human being who is very much like you, without the title.

That's why it is so important to spend a bulk of your time on working on the relationship component of the 7 Essential Traits of Leadership.

And notice where Directorship falls ... at the end of the 7 traits. It's not a coincidence.

TAKEAWAYS

Leadership is Directorship : _____

_____

_____

_____

_____

_____

_____

SUMMARY

You may have read this book in one sitting, skimmed it, or taken your time to go through, but however you did it, you are here.

Now what?

Where do you go from here?

First, let us summarize some of what you hopefully discovered. The following blank lines are for you to jot some of your takeaways from the book.

After the takeaway section, I share some very important information I want you to take note of. Don't overlook them. So keep reading.

TAKEAWAYS

Influential Leaders, Different Outcomes:____

_____

_____

_____

_____

_____

_____

188 | KINGSLEY GRANT

Better Decisions, Better Outcomes: _____

_____

_____

_____

_____

_____

_____

Lead from Position or with Permission:

_____

_____

_____

_____

_____

_____

Emotions Matter: _____

_____

_____

_____

_____

_____

_____

Self-Awareness and Leadership: _____

_____

_____

_____

_____

_____

Social Awareness and Leadership: _____

_____

_____

_____

_____

_____

_____

Leadership Has a Price: _____

_____

_____

_____

_____

_____

_____

Leadership is Stewardship: _____

_____

_____

_____

_____

_____

_____

Leadership is Relationship: _____

_____

_____

_____

_____

_____

_____

Leadership is Partnership: _____

_____

_____

_____

_____

_____

_____

Leadership is Mentorship: _____

_____

_____

_____

_____

_____

_____

Leadership is Craftsmanship: _____

_____

_____

_____

_____

_____

_____

Leadership is Salesmanship: _____

_____

_____

_____

_____

_____

_____

Leadership is Directorship: _____

_____

_____

_____

_____

_____

_____

ONE LAST THING

I have created a digest page of some of the posts I've made on social media and, because of the number of engagements on the posts, I chose the ones that I believe summarize the Emotelligent Leader. You'll find those in the next section.

Secondly, I've prepared a page entitled, "Pledge of the Emotelligent Leader." This is what I had referenced in the early section of the book.

I would like for you to make your pledge to join me and others who are going to operate in our lives as leaders in a way that make our world better. This we will do by helping those entrusted to us become their best selves.

From this point on, I want you to think of yourself as an Emotelligent Leader when you find yourself in situations that trigger you negatively and use your emotional intelligence to respond in a way that shows you are in charge of your emotions as well as those around you.

Lastly, if you found great value in what you have read, I would very much like for you to do the following:

1. Spread the word

2. Leave your honest feedback on Amazon

3. Invite me to speak at your next leadership event as a trainer or keynote speaker

4. Hire me as your leadership coach or your company's leadership consultant

5. Sign up on my website at www.kingsleygrant.com for updates and other leadership-related information

6. Now, go out and show the world, especially your tribe, what it means to be an Emotelligent Leader. Let's make the world a better place through this leadership paradigm.

You're now the leader everybody is going to love and want to follow. You will succeed where others failed.

EMOTELLIGENT LEADERSHIP CHEAT SHEET

1.

_____ ADVANCE DIGNITY AND AGENGA _____

A good leader thinks about how he or she can make decisions that not only promotes the agenda of the company or organization but also the value and dignity of the employee.

Leaders who focuses only on the agenda of the company or organization at the expense of their people will suffer loss.

- Loss of productivity.

- Loss of talented people

- Loss of profits, etc.

As important as it is to advance the agenda of the organization or company, so it is in advancing the dignity and value of the workers.

2.

_____ A SMILE _____

As a leader, make sure your body language is one that says, "I'm approachable" and mean it. Your team deserves that much and more. Try smiling. It helps.

I've noticed that some leaders default to a stern facial expression around their team thinking that this gets them more respect and drives fear into their people.

This is simply ignorance and maybe arrogance on their part. It's obvious they do not understand human motivation.

198 | KINGSLEY GRANT

3.

_____ BE THE THERMOSTATIC LEADER _____

As a leader, it's your responsibility to be the thermostat and set the emotional temperature for your team. You then become the thermometer, monitoring to make sure it remains comfortable for all.

The emotional temperature determines the level of productivity arising from the workplace.

It's your responsibility as a leader to make sure the right temperature is set and then monitor to make sure it remains that way.

Skillful leadership is required to set and maintain the right setting. Unfortunately, not all leaders are equipped to lead this way.

4.

_____ THEY CHOSE YOU _____

Treat your people in a way that make them feel appreciated. Remember, at the end of the day, they chose to work in your company. Something about your company attracted them.

It is your responsibility to not disappoint them by treating them as disposable objects.

Therefore, do your best to continually communicate your gratitude and appreciation.

5.

_____ CONGRUENCY _____

The Emotelligent Leader understands that people trust what they see over what they hear so they seek to align both.

It's hard to lead when what you're saying is being contradicted by what you're showing.

Make every effort to bring them into alignment.

6.

_____ WHAT'S RIGHT OR WHO'S RIGHT _____

The Emotelligent Leader makes being right a secondary goal to finding a resolution.

Far too many people focus on wanting to be right, which is understandable. However, the Emotelligent Leader helps people to look at WHAT'S right rather than who is right.

7.

_____ IT'S MUTUAL _____

The Emotelligent Leader understands that he/she is responsible for 50% of the success of a relationship. So, they work hard at doing their part and help others do the same.

Some people directly or indirectly place the burden of a relationship success on one party. They seek to exclude themselves especially when there has been a breach in the relationship.

This mindset makes it almost impossible to have a healthy and vibrant relationship in the home, the marketplace, or wherever relationships are experienced.

8.
_____ MADE A MISTAKE _____

The Emotelligent Leader understands that mistakes do not define but refine a person. They help them with the latter.

All of us have made mistakes or will make mistakes. When we do, we want to be shown mercy.

Give your team room to make mistakes and then gracefully and lovingly walk them through to a place of forgiveness. Help them to learn from their mistakes.

9.
_____ WHY THEY LEFT _____

Companies and organizations lose some of their best talent, not because of the company or organization per se, but because of poor or unskilled leadership.

Many companies and organizations lose some of their best talented people to their competition, not because of a better offer, but simply because their leaders were unskilled in the area of EI.

One study by the Center of Creative Leadership confirmed this dynamic of failed leadership — a deficit in emotional competence.

10.

_____ SEEK TO REWARD _____

As a leader, make it a habit to catch your people doing what's right and reward them rather than wait for them to do what's wrong and punish them.

One of the most important habits we should cultivate, especially as leaders, is the reward habit.

Unfortunately, most leaders fail at this. They are more apt to lean to the "Punish Habit." Their people only hear from them when they mess up.

What if you as a leader made it a habit to focus more on looking for opportunities to reward the behavior you wanted more of? I guarantee you would have a team that gives you more than you ask for. Try it.

11.

_____ THEY WILL IF YOU KNOW HOW _____

The greatest task of a leader is not to get people to work, it's to get them to *want* to work. Emotelligent Leaders know how.

Some leaders have a difficult time getting their troop to be more productive. They have tried different methods but still not moved the needle.

Research shows that the best method to increase productivity is to develop your EQ skills.

202 | KINGSLEY GRANT

12.

_____ LEADERSHIP BLOOPER _____

Most managers in the workforce were promoted because they were good at what they did, and not necessarily good at making the people around them better.

One of the mistakes that organizations and companies make is promoting based on someone's time with the company or simply on performance.

Even though both are good considerations, they're not the best criteria.

Having effective leadership training is paramount to the organization's success.

13.

_____ THEY DO JUST ENOUGH _____

I find that people leave their best selves outside of the workplace simply because leaders fail to give them reasons otherwise.

So many companies and organizations operate at a "less than" level when it comes to productivity and they can't figure out why.

One of the main reasons is that they fail to recognize what people need most to give their best selves.

14.

_____ IT'S A REASONS GAME _____

Research by Gallup found that 87 percent of workers show up to work because they have to. What if Leaders could get them to show up to work because they want to?

In the sales world, you'll hear the term "it's a numbers game." The reasoning is that the more you pitch, the better the chance of getting a sale. It's all about the numbers.

In the workplace, it's all about the reasons. The more reasons you give your team to want to perform, the better the chance they will.

However, there's one reason above all else that employees cite as the most motivating (drum roll) .... acknowledgement

15.

_____ PROMOTION / HIRE BLUNDER _____

If you want to kill an organization, kill productivity, kill morale within an organization, hire the wrong leader or promote the wrong person.

I've found this to be so true, both in my experience as an employee as well as in my role as a leadership consultant and trainer.

My suggestion to organizations is to hire and / or promote carefully. Make sure you evaluate for high EI.

In fact, nearly three-quarters (71 percent) of hiring managers surveyed by Career Builder in 2011 said they valued an employee's emotional quotient or EQ over their IQ. A further three-quarter (75 percent) said they would be more likely to promote an employee with high emotional intelligence. And, get this? More than half (59 percent) said they wouldn't hire a candidate with a high IQ and low EQ.

204 | KINGSLEY GRANT

16.

__ AUTHORITY IS A WEAK LEADERSHIP SKILL __

Some people confuse having authority as leadership. You can use authority to get people to do as you say but that's the most you'll get from them. They reserve their best selves for real leaders.

Some leaders use the authority card to get their people to work. It does work but it does not inspire or motivate. It does the opposite.

This approach is a reflection of poor leadership skills.

17.

_____ TRY PUTTING MORE IN _____

Your role as a leader is to seek to put more into your people than seek to get more out of them. The former leads to the latter.

So many leaders wonder why they're not getting the most out of their team. They've tried various techniques, both manipulative and seemingly non-manipulative, yet to no avail.

What they're missing is that most important ingredient: PUT MORE IN. You cannot get OUT what you've not put IN.

What you put IN to your team is crucial for your company or organizational success.

18.

_____ MAKE IT SAFE _____

Research shows that when a leader does his or her best to make their team members feel safe, their members will do everything in their power to make their vision and mission successful.

As a leader, make it your priority to create a safe environment where your people can spend less of their energy on self-preservation.

An "unsafe" environment can add unnecessary and avoidable stress to your team because they have to worry about what they say, making mistakes, and retribution from management.

ABOUT THE AUTHOR

Kingsley Grant, M.S., is a national and international speaker whose transformational talks have helped high-performing leaders make better decisions, have better relationships, and have a greater influence.

He has been referred to by some as "a leader of leaders" and has coached and trained a number of leaders with his Hybrid approach to Leadership - a mixture of Emotional Intelligence and Leadership skills.

He is the author of the #1 Amazon Best Seller: The Midlife Launch - successfully pursue your dreams without giving up what's most important to you. He has written several other books and e-books that can be found on Amazon.

Kingsley is a psychotherapist, focusing on Marriage and Family Therapy. He received his training at St. Thomas University in Miami, Florida. He graduated at the top of his class as a Cum Laude student.

He is the first member of his family to have obtained a Master's Degree.

208 | KINGSLEY GRANT

Kingsley is passionate about taking his message of hope to as many people as possible. This passion is real within him because of his desire for people to not take their dreams to the graveyard.

He believes the graveyard is enriched enough with dreams that were never realized. This became a mission of his even more so after the death of his mom who "secretly" desired to be a nurse, but never became one. She spent her adult life as a teacher, fulfilling as it was, yet the nurse within her never been given a chance. It went to the graveyard with her.

Kingsley is also a heart surgery survivor who believes God has kept him here to help people become their best selves. He tags himself as the Hope Dispenser and the Graveyard Robber. These monikers remind him of his mission on earth.

He believes that leadership is the best way to influence others. So, he focuses on helping leaders lead in a way that gives them the best chance of succeeding where others may have failed.

Kingsley is available for leadership consulting, coaching, and training. The best way to know more about him is through his website: www.kingsleygrant.com. Here you'll be able to contact him to schedule him for speaking, consulting, or coaching.

PLEDGE OF THE EMOTELLIGENT LEADER

As an Emotelligent Leader, I _____
pledge to incorporate the 7 Essential Traits of
Leadership into my role as a leader. In addition, I will:

1.   Manage my emotions and not let them manage me

2.   Manage my relationships through the lens of Self and Social Awareness

3.   Be swift to hear and slow to speak

4.   Make it more about them and less about me

5.   Seek to serve and not to be served

6.   Seek to understand more than to be understood

7.   Make what's right a priority over who is right

8.   Be quick to say I'm sorry, I was wrong, please forgive me

9.   Give others the benefit of the doubt

10. Treat others as I want to be treated

Signature: _____

Date: _____

BUILD YOUR EMOTIONAL VOCABULARY

AFRAID	HURT	SAD
• Fearful	• Crushed	• Tearful
• Terrified	• Pained	• Sorrowful
• Suspicious	• Offended	• Pained
• Anxious	• Heartbroken	• Grief
• Nervous	• Agonized	• Anguish
• Scared	• Deprived	• Desperate
• Worried	• Rejected	• Unhappy
• Frightened	• Dejected	• Lonely
• Timid	• Appalled	• Grieved

BUILD YOUR EMOTIONAL VOCABULARY
(cont'd)

LOVE	HAPPY	GOOD
• Loving	• Great	• Calm
• Considerate	• Joyous	• Peaceful
• Affectionate	• Elated	• Content
• Tender	• Important	• Certain
• Attracted	• Ecstatic	• Reassured
• Warm	• Glad	• Pleased
• Comforted(ing)	• Cheerful	• Encouraged
• Devoted	• Satisfied	• Relaxed
• Loved	• Overjoyed	• Hopeful

SOURCES

Chapter 3: Better Decisions Better Outcomes

A. Smith. (2018, November 22). The Miracle On The Hudson: how it happened. Retrieved from https://www.telegraph.co.uk/films/sully/miracle-on-the-hudson-how-it-happened/

Talent Smart (2019). Retrieved from http://www.talentsmart.com/

Chapter 4: Position or Permission Leadership

Maxwell, John C. (2013, October 13). John C. Maxwell on Influence. Retrieved from https://www.youtube.com/watch?v=ROh9vkyK9uA

Chapter 8: Leadership Has A Price

Whitten, Sarah (2018, April 16). Starbucks manager who called police on two black men has left the company. Retrieved from https://www.cnbc.com/2018/04/16/starbucks-manager-who-called-police-on-two-black-men-has-left-the-company-.html?recirc=taboolainternal

Gallup (2013): State of the Global Workplace, Retrieved from https://www.gallup.com/services/178517/state-global-workplace.aspx

Chapter 9: Leadership is Stewardship

Clay, Rebecca A. (2015, September). The changing workplace. Retrieved from https://www.apa.org/monitor/2015/09/workplace

Safe Work Australia website (2016, November, 23rd). Psychosocial safety climate and better productivity in Australian workplaces: Costs, productivity, presenteeism, absenteeism. Retrieved from https://www.safeworkaustralia.gov.au/doc/psychosocial-safety-climate-and-better-productivity-australian-workplaces-costs-productivity

MultiVu (2019) New Cigna Study Reveals Loneliness at Epidemic Levels in America. Retrieved from https://www.multivu.com/players/English/8294451-cigna-us-loneliness-survey/

National Health Service website (2015, March, 13th). Loneliness, increase risk of premature death. Retrieved from https://www.nhs.uk/news/mental-health/loneliness-increases-risk-of-premature-death/

Novotney, Amy (2017, November). Trends report: Research zeroes in on the costs of unhealthy workplaces. Retrieved from https://www.apa.org/monitor/2017/11/trends-workplaces

Platzer, Erich (2014, May, 23rd). 1000% ROI By Recruiting Emotionally Intelligent Managers. Retrieved from https://www.performance-effect.com/growth-by-sales-team-with-high-emotional-competencies/

McCreary, Matthew (2018, September, 25th). Chick-fil-A Makes More Per Restaurant Than McDonald's, Starbucks and Subway Combined ... and It's Closed on Sundays. Retrieved from https://www.entrepreneur.com/article/320615

Genos International (2015, April, 14th). Improving Sales Revenue – Sanofi-Aventis. Retrieved from https://www.genosinternational.com/improving-sales-revenue/

Chapter 10: Designing A Safe Culture

Revesencio, Jonha (2015, July, 7th) Why Happy Employees Are 12% More Productive. Retrieved from https://www.fastcompany.com/3048751/happy-employees-are-12-more-productive-at-work

O.C.Tanner Institute (2019). Retrieved from http://www.octanner.com

Chapter 12: Leadership is Partnership

Mautz, Scott (2017, May, 11th). Psychology and Neuroscience Blow-Up the Myth of Effective Multitasking. Retrieved from https://www.inc.com/scott-mautz/psychology-and-neuroscience-blow-up-the-myth-of-effective-multitasking.html

Chapter 14: Leadership is Craftsmanship

Kalla, Susan (2012, May, 31st). Keys to Excellence (Even Michael Jordan Had to Do It). Retrieved from https://www.forbes.com/sites/susankalla/2012/05/31/six-keys-to-excellence-at-anything/#605a8bc822f2

Chapter 15: Leadership is Salesmanship

Deutshendorf, Harvey (2015, June, 15th). Why Emotionally Intelligent People Are More Successful. Retrieved from

(https://www.fastcompany.com/3047455/why-emotionally-intelligent-people-are-more-successful)

Chernis, Cary (2019). The Business Case Emotional Intelligence. Retrieved from http://www.eiconsortium.org/reports/business_case_for_ei.html

Chapter 16: Leadership is Directorship

Genesis 3:1-19 (New Living Translation)

www.ingramcontent.com/pod-product-compliance
Lightning Source LLC
Chambersburg PA
CBHW052128270326
41930CB00012B/2803